Bringing Our Angel Home

Other books by Tracy Sanford Pillow:

Max's Adoption
(ISBN 0-595-13003-8, $9.99 USA) ($15.95 CAN)
Adventures in Special-Needs Adoption!
a foster care success story

Where Do Freckles Come From?
(ISBN 0-595-12051-2, $9.99 USA) ($15.99 CAN)
A Delightful Rhyming Children's Book!
whimsical answers for a very persistent little girl

Bharat Mata
As Humanity Unfolds in Mother India
(ISBN 0-595-18203-8, $10.95 USA) ($17.95 CAN)
I will never forget the little ones I held, rocked, and played with.
I will never forget the despair and hopelessness I've seen, felt, and heard.
I will never forget the little band of Christians there
striving to exist in a harsh, corrupt environment.
I will never forget the India I experienced
because the eyes and smiles of the kids
traveled home with me, in my heart!

Bringing Our Angel Home

Tracy Sanford Pillow

Writers Club Press
San Jose New York Lincoln Shanghai

Bringing Our Angel Home

Writers Club Press
an imprint of iUniverse, Inc.

For information address:
iUniverse, Inc.
5220 S. 16th St., Suite 200
Lincoln, NE 68512
www.iuniverse.com

ISBN: 0-595-22442-3

Printed in the United States of America

-to Joan-

*Joan was never distressed about Minh's glaring imperfections, only seeing an endearing little cherub spirit with deep longings for tenderness and generosity. She served as Minh's **second mama** from the day we brought her home.*

*My only regret is that since we've moved, I won't get to be there with an open heart and arms for her daughter when she's brought **home** from China in a few months.*

The soul is dyed the color of its
thoughts. Think only on those things
that are in line with your principles
and can bear the full light of day.
The content of your character
is your choice. Day by day, what you
choose, what you think, and what you do
is who you become. Your integrity is
your destiny…it is the light
that guides your way.

*(I have no idea who penned this
or even where I first read it,
but I rely on its message daily.)*

Contents

Acknowledgements

I want to extend my heart-felt gratitude to
Lutheran Service Society of Western Pennsylvania
and **Holt International Children's Services**
for helping us bring our daughter home.

Introduction

As I flip through the glossy pages of a magazine, *I see her eyes*…I turn back to get a closer look and I'm drawn in by her expression of humility and grace. *When I peer closer, I see a quiet, desperate pleading.*

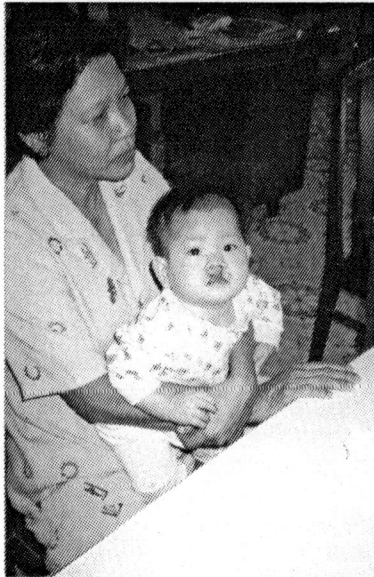

The magazine is **Hi Families**, a publication of Holt International Children's Services. I show my family the photo of the little one (*Minh*) from the "Waiting Children" section and they also sense a familiar tug at their hearts. **We agree that God has sent this little angel,** *however indirectly,* **straight to us.**

We get on the phone to Holt and ask about Minh. *How do we go about bringing her* **home**? They explain the process and we immediately get to work. *There's not a doubt in my mind that this little girl half-way* *across the world is my daughter.* I have both birth and adopted children. **A *mama* just knows! *Her heart tells her!***

Children are gifts from God. When I give birth, the miracle of it all leaves me no doubt that God has entrusted me personally with this new little one to love and care for. It's the same with adoption. *God is in the process.* Although brought into the world by another, he bestows upon me a gift, a precious child. The maternal feelings are the same, very strong, and just as natural.

Minh has been waiting, *waiting* for almost 2 years for her mama to find her.

Paperwork and More Paperwork

Since we know and have seen the child we wish to adopt, the first part of our process is a little different. Usually you get a child referral months after completing the home study. We're working a little backwards.

We apply to Holt to be considered for Minh's **forever family**. We fill out a formal application requesting Vietnam as our country of choice and Minh as our child. About a week before Thanksgiving, we get word that we've been chosen. Holt sends a referral to a local adoption agency, Lutheran Service Society of Western Pennsylvania, to begin the home study process.

We call Lutheran because we're so anxious to get started. The holidays are fast approaching and we'd like to at least get one required home visit done before we head to Tennessee for Thanksgiving. Shirley Mitchell, the social worker assigned our case, calls and we choose dates for the required home visits.

The **home study** is the single most important document in the entire adoption process. Shirley comes to our home and asks questions designed to sincerely get to know the family, *the prospective parents and siblings*. Just some of the issues covered in this process are our motivation to adopt, the family background of the prospective parents, education, health and employment history of both parents, description of other family members in the home as well as extended family, our marital relationship, discipline management, attitudes towards adoption, our community, finances, references...Finally, Shirley has to compile all of this information and make a recommendation. *Are we prepared and suitable for the child we wish to adopt?*

◆   ◆   ◆

I think a little background information is needed. Jimmy and I were highschool sweethearts, now married for 16 years. We went to college together in middle Tennessee and eagerly started having children immediately upon graduation. Jimmy is a soldier in the U.S. Army Medical Service Corps and because of his career, we've had the opportunity to live in various locations—Texas, Germany, Georgia, Tennessee, Pennsylvania…and now Montana. I've held various positions, received my Master's degree in 1998, and now write books, magazine articles, and love taking photos.

◆   ◆   ◆

In preparation for the first home visit, of course we threaten our four children to be on their best behavior. *HA!* Our oldest, Caleb, is almost 13! He's very compassionate, musical, *and big and sturdy like a Tonka*. Next comes Lucas, turning 11 years old next month. He's our creative, *tall and blonde* wild child! Morgan recently turned 8. She's our amber-haired, freckle face daughter who is feisty yet sweet, *and enduringly nurturing*. Our youngest, Max, is our *7 year-old ball of energy*! He has huge blue eyes and the deepest dimples ever seen on a little one. Well, I should have spent more time preparing our puppies instead of worrying about our children. The children answer her questions honestly and intelligently. Midway through our talk, *Skippy and Chiklet*, our two wild puppies, burst through the door *I think I have them locked in*, run in, and jump all over Shirley, *licking and yelping*!?!?

Our second home visit goes quite well, *until…*The children **and** puppies are acting great. The big boys are downstairs and I put a movie in upstairs in the master bedroom for Morgan and Max so Jimmy and

I can talk with Shirley, uninterrupted. The little ones sure are being quiet back there. *Quiet isn't always a good thing.* In walks Morgan and Max with little film canisters of teeth. *They've obviously been snooping non-stop in our bedroom.* They've found my individually-labeled canisters containing their baby teeth. Morgan asks how we got them!?!? *"What are these teeth doing in your panty drawer? Those look like the same teeth the Tooth Fairy took when she left money on her late night visits!"* Jimmy and I look at each other. Shirley looks at us. *She can't wait to see our parenting skills in action! What do we do?* **I lie.** I tell Morgan that after the Tooth Fairy takes the teeth from under their pillows, she leaves them with us for souvenirs!?!? Jimmy takes the snoopers back to the bedroom and gives them the sternest look he can conjure up while telling them to watch the movie for just 30 more minutes, *and stay out of our drawers!*

Through all the shenanigans, Shirley makes a positive recommendation and we go on from there. First, we submit required documents to Immigration. Next is the **dossier** process. All of the paperwork looks *depressingly daunting* but we start at the beginning and plow our way through, step by step.

I don't just collect the usual documents. Each piece has to be signed, notarized, and state certified. The documents include: a Vietnamese application for adoption and commitment form (all in the foreign language—*we just sign and date…*), certified birth certificates as well as the *TN-certified ribboned and gold-sealed* marriage certificate, a letter from our physician stating that we have no infectious diseases including HIV and AIDS and no mental disorders *(close call at this point, HA!)*, photocopies of our passports, employment letters revealing our exact income, the *all-important* home study and home study synopsis, photocopy of Immigration approvals, a couple of power of attorneys, police clearances from our local law department, family photographs, and 6 passport photos each. It may not sound like very much, *but believe me*, it takes some time and effort to gather all of this. Once this is all notarized, Jimmy treks to our capital, Harrisburg, Pennsylvania, to hand-deliver the documents to be state certified. Once the various certifications and rubber stamps are completed, we're instructed to make five complete copies of this huge stack, send 4 to Holt and keep 1 for our records. Holt reviews for accuracy then forwards them to Vietnam for **authentication**.

A short time later, we receive **Pham Tam Minh's** legal documents—birth certificate, minutes of her abandonment, Vietnamese relinquishment for adoption, her initial social history...*all on delicate longer-style European paper written in Vietnamese.*

A U.S. immigrant visa is required for each child being adopted from abroad. Because we've received Minh's legal documents, we now file the petition for the next phase of this visa process at the INS (Immigration and Naturalization Service) office in Pittsburgh. We take her legal documents, the petition (*Petition to Clarify Orphan as an Immediate Relative*), a check, and instructions for INS to cable their visa petition decision directly to the American Consulate in Ho Chi Minh City, Vietnam.

After filing the petition, we gather documents for the last *immigrant visa* phase which is an interview that will take place in Vietnam. Required documents are the homestudy, certified birth and marriage certificates for both of us, copy of the 1st phase's application and approval letter, an Affidavit of Support, original letters of employment, our last 3 years' tax returns with original W-2s, and finally, an affidavit concerning immigration vaccination waivers.

◆   ◆   ◆

The Initial Social History describes the details of her abandonment. **She's abandoned close to the Binh Duong child welfare center/ orphanage on 24 July 1999.** Mrs. Lieu, a worker for the Rural Water Supply Project, finds her right after midnight and takes her into the orphanage.

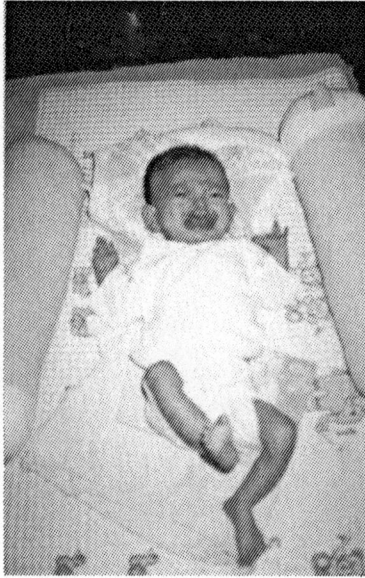

Once inside, they examine her. Most noticeable is her cleft lip and palate, which they refer to as *harelip*. It states that she's very weak, pale, and malnourished. She has a severe case of scabies. They try to feed her milk but she vomits. They feed her milk by spoon. Because of her black hair and eyes *and the shape of her eyes*, they note that her race is **Kinh**. When sleeping, she prefers to lie on her stomach, sucking her fingers. She can turn on her side and roll over from her back to her stomach.

◆   ◆   ◆

We make it our foremost mission to find out as much as possible about cleft lip and palate…the whys, whens, hows, the what nexts… A cleft is a separation of the parts of the lip or roof of the mouth which usually come together during the early weeks in the development of an unborn child. A cleft lip is a separation of the two sides of the lip and often includes the bones of the upper jaw (**maxilla**) and the upper gum (**alveolar ridge**). It looks like there's a split in the lip and upper gum. A cleft lip can range from a slight notch in the red portion of the lips (**vermilion**) to a complete separation of the lip extending into and distorting the tip and side (**ala**) of the nose. When there's a cleft lip, frequently the upper gum (**alveolar ridge**) is also separated. Clefts of the lip may occur on one or both sides, with varying degrees of severity. If the cleft occurs on one side, it's called a unilateral cleft lip. It the cleft occurs on both sides of the lip, it's called a bilateral cleft lip, *like Minh's*.

No single cause of cleft lip, cleft palate, or both has been identified. The majority of clefts seem to be due to a combination of genes probably interacting with certain environmental factors. Clefting occurs very early in a pregnancy and represents a problem over which a pregnant woman probably has no control. Clefts of the lip and palate are among the most common of all birth defects. While cleft palate seems to occur in all racial groups equally, cleft lip with or without cleft palate, is most common in Asians. It's less common in whites, and least common in blacks. I'm surprised to discover that one out of every 700 to 750 infants born alive in the United States has a cleft lip and/or palate.

◆   ◆   ◆

The orphanage staff undress her and write that her current weight is 8kg and height is 68cm. **While undressed, they see writing on her arm.** It reads ***Pham Tam Minh*** and in Vietnamese, ***3 May 1999,*** *her assumed birthdate.* So, she's approximately 3 months old. Usually babies are abandoned at birth, but her parents obviously love her and try to keep her. No doubt it's impossible for them to get her the medical attention she desperately needs, so in the end *they love enough to give her up.* The name they gift her with means "*bright, clear mind.*" They want her rescuers to know that if you look past her physical deformity, she has intelligence and a compassionate heart. ***How their hearts must shatter when they gentle place her on the ground and give her one last kiss before turning away!*** The caregivers also take notes of her scars, *that were evidently intentional.* On both ears on the back of the curves are matching 5mm crescent moons. She also has a small crescent-shaped scar on her bottom lip.

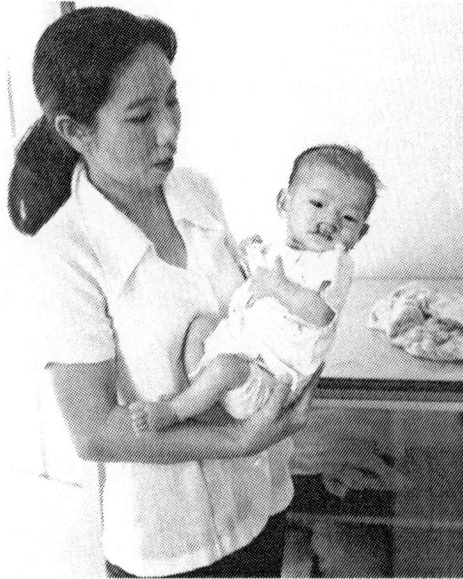

Getting To Know Our Little Girl

Holt sends periodic reports straight from the orphanage. They're so fun to read and we learn a lot about Minh through these papers. Their limited English, or the translations from Vietnamese gives situations all new meanings at times.

From the sound of the report dated 10 May 2000, Minh is living with a foster family, *Nguyen Thi Trang*. She is 1 year, 1 month old. Her present weight is 9kg, height 70cm. It states that she still has difficulty eating. She often vomits when eating, *but enjoys food and likes to eat a lot*. She has 3 meals a day of rice soup, along with milk a few times a day. She sleeps well, almost 10 hours of uninterrupted sleep at night. She also takes 2 naps, one in the morning and another in the afternoon.

She gets *"inflammation of the lung"* and is hospitalized 3 April for 8 days. They test her for Hepatitis B, with a negative result. She cuts 2 teeth on the bottom. Immunizations are started.

The report says that she can sit without support and stand up for a moment. She crawls fast. She pulls herself up to stand. She understands what people say. It also reveals that Minh is attached to her foster mother. She *"distinguishes strangers or familiars."* She likes to cuddle. *"She cries when is unpleasing."* The foster mother writes that she sucks two fingers, likes someone to talk to her, and to be carried around.

They're looking for an adoptive family, overseas. Although the report is dated 10 May 2000, we get it much later. After we're chosen to be her new parents, they send us **all** of the available reports, *to catch us up with her life*. Through Holt, we send her stickers, coloring books and crayons.

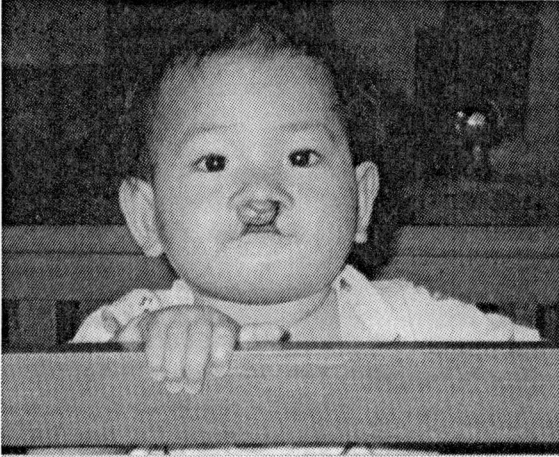

◆   ◆   ◆

The next report on 15 August 2000 shows that Minh is healthy. She's living in the orphanage full-time now. It makes no mention of the reason she no longer lives with the foster family. She doesn't get sick in the last 3 months. She weighs 9.5kg and is 73cm tall. She's seen by a doctor's assistant named Pham Tuyet Trinh. She's spoon-fed milk and lies back on the floor twice a day for her soup to be poured in. The soup is soft rice cooked with meat and potatoes. For a snack, she has yogurt. She's now 1 year, 3 months. It says *"the child often get salivation due to her lift-palate and hare lips."* She has another bout of scabies.

Minh has good motor skills. She can sit stable and starts walking on 26 July 2000. She also carries toys when walking. She cuts 1 tooth on her upper jaw in the flesh/gum protruding from her nose and 2 teeth on the bottom. *"Minh began to gurgle sound to express her joy, to ask for food or to call for attention."*

The report says that she's happy but *"shows much fear when she commits mistake."* Minh imitates the caregivers when waving good-bye. She cooperates when dressing in the morning. *"The child needs attention from people thus she pretended to cry to catch attention of people for holding her. When not being held, she would cry long-lastingly."* She remembers her foster mother *"thus she showed her happiness when her foster mother visited her."*

The report states that they still actively search for her a suitable family. It says *"the child needs a family who committed for special medical care for the child since she is suffering by harelip and left palate."* It goes on to say ***"The joyful child shows that she is a bright and lovely child thus her adoptive family will be satisfied about her."***

◆   ◆   ◆

The report dated 12 November 2000 describes Minh as relatively healthy, gaining centimeters (now 75cm tall) and weight (10.5kg). Although the report is dated Nov 2000, we get it around Dec/Jan 2001. She does have another bout of *"inflammation of lung"* and is hospitalized from 11 to 14 September. The medicines administered are Biodroxil, Exomuc, and Chlophenirmin. I immediately fax this information to our pediatrician (Dr. Kathy Lopez, Sewickley) to give her some idea of her condition and treatments. She also receives the immunization for Japanese cerebritis in October.

There's a lot of information in this report. It says that she has good motor skills which they explain in broken English. She can walk through the corridor of the orphanage. She can *"grasp things with her hands firmly."* Minh can stand up from a sitting position and walk down the stairs. *"The child walk to the bathroom to get her towel. She can take off her pant."* She can comb her hair with a little comb even though *"it is not so skillful."* About her speech, it states she *"is learning to speak hard due to her hare lips…However, the child becomes to pronounce gurgle sounds."*

Always under Social and Emotional Development, it notes *"the child grows faster than her age in this area."* She can take her pants off and bring them to the sink after the caretaker asks her just once. Minh loves to be held so she follows adults around. Our daughter, Morgan, loves the part in this section where it says that she likes her hair to be brushed and brushed. ***"After the caretakers brushed her hair, she stands in front of the mirror to look at herself and smiles interestingly."*** So, she primps like her big sis.

The neatest information is Minh's love for music that's revealed. We're a very musical family and it's a big part of our lives. **I'm so happy that Minh has already discovered a love for music as well.** It says Minh often jumps up and down holding the edge of the crib when listening to music. *"The child likes listening to music very much…often dances when hearing music."* It goes on to say that she's very happy when people talk to her and hold her. *"Minh is an emotional child thus she needs to have attention from adults."* It says that she has a good appetite, likes sweet potatoes the best. *"She often makes wet when sleeping."* They stress the need for an adoptive family and surgery as soon as possible. ***"This family-oriented child will develop very well in a loving family."***

Right after receiving this and reading it a bunch of times, we go and buy her a funky little hand mirror, cute clippies for her hair, and a cassette with lively music that has children singing favorites. We send it to Holt and they forward it on to the orphanage.

◆   ◆   ◆

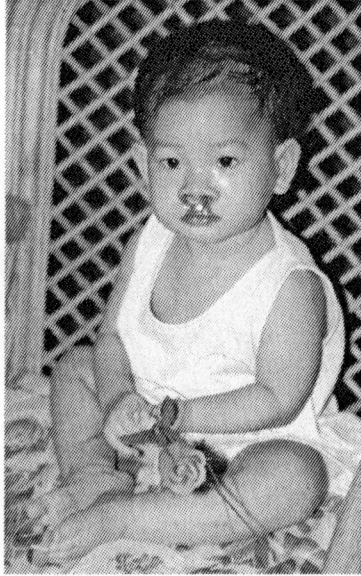

The next update (10 February 2001) describes another hospitalization from 22-25 November 2000 for *"inflammation of lung."* This time, the medicine administered includes Augmentin, Presnisolon, and Exomuc. Other than that, she's described as healthy. She still has a bowl of rice soup, but now cooked with fish twice a day, and yogurt for a snack. It doesn't mention milk. She's now 77cm tall and weighs 11kg.

Her personality really comes through when you read between the lines. She seems to be quite a character! We're partial to intelligent children, *with a little feisty fire thrown in.* She can walk along the corridor and up stairs at the orphanage. *"She can throw balls and push a baby carriage."* It goes on to say that ***"the child often stands on her tiptoe to pull the curtains down"...HA!..."can carry a small chair running around the room."*** Of course she still has problems with speech. She does make great efforts to express herself. *"Minh* *understands all instruction of her caregivers."* It doesn't say if she actually listens though.

She can dress herself and wash and dry her hands when dirty. *"The child is attached to Mr. Binh."* He's the regional director. *"She identifies him as a very close friend and is happy playing with him."* It goes on to say *"the child often looks for him at the end of the working time since she knows that at that time he can play with her longer."* Le Binh has a room there on the orphanage property. The report notes that she likes playing with the other babies in the nursery.

She *"tries to be"* obedient and is very intelligent. Minh has a good appetite *"and makes progress in trying not to get wet at night."* I laugh when I read *"the child likes cool air and loves staying in the one office equipped with air conditioner,"* Mr. Binh's. She's smart!?!?

At the end, it notes that ***"everyone loves her...despite being a handicapped child, she wins the heart of all people in the center through her wonderful open personality."*** We can't wait to finally go get her and bring her home to be a part of our family. It sounds like she's going to fit right in!

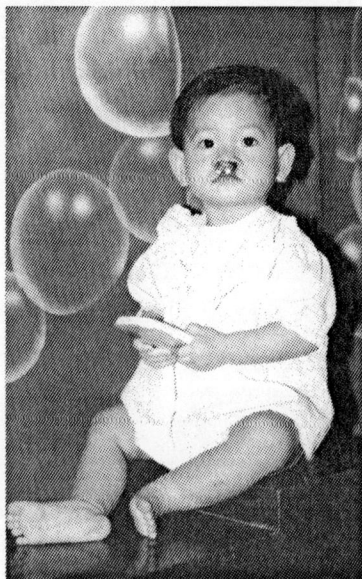

◆   ◆   ◆

The last update report we get is dated 10 April 2001. Of course she has grown over the last couple of months, 4cm taller and gaining 0.5kg. She has cut 2 more teeth. She now has 9 teeth, 4 upper and 5 lower. We're a little worried because it notes that she doesn't have a good appetite lately, probably due to the weather. The climate is tropical but in the summer time the heat rises to burning proportions. For her 2 main meals, she has a bowl of soft rice cooked with fish, eel, and vegetables. She now has soft fruit after the noon naptime.

She walks on the tip of her toes in the nursery. She likes to try and jump. When requested, she'll stand on one foot. She climbs out of her crib. Minh still likes playing ball, kicking and throwing. *"The child begins to take off her shirt."* I don't blame her. It's hot! She beats the back of the cabinets to make different sounds. *"The child holds pen to draw on paper. However, she cannot shape her drawing yet."*

The update goes on to say that she doesn't fear strangers but approaches them to be held. She still adores music. I find these sentences pretty funny: **"She loves to be beautiful thus she imitates adults to brush her hair and then look at herself in the mirror"**…and…**"tries to get the hearts of caretakers in the orphanage thus she beats children who were complained by her caretaker."** They send the cutest photo of her all dressed up with the clippies we sent her in her hair. She's also holding the mirror and music cassette in the photo. *It makes me feel more connected somehow.* She definitely sounds like fun! She also loves sneaking outside of her nursery room to play with adults.

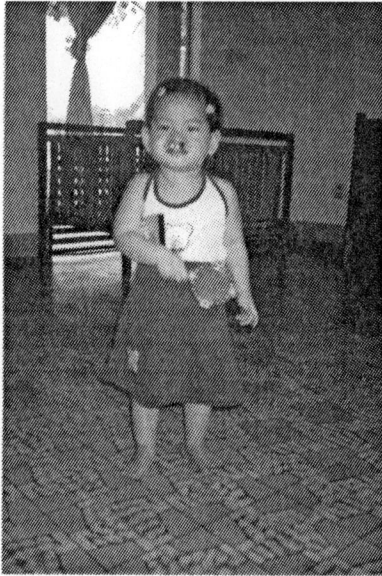

It says Minh likes playing with stuffed toys and making friends with people. *"She is an intelligent child thus she seldom punished by her caretakers though she is a bit naughty."* She still likes sweet potatoes best of all, often asking to eat. *"Tam Minh will be a very successful child in the future if she has an appropriate education."*

We get really excited when we read in her Needs section , that *"she needs to be prepared for placement."* The Plan Intervention is to *"make her familiar with her adoptive family."* The last sentence describes the Permanency Plan which reveals that Minh is waiting for departure (assigned to the Pillows) *"with an implementation date of May-June 2001."* **What does this mean?**

I get right on the phone and call Sara at Holt. I ask her if it's true that we could get travel approval as early as May, as the paper dictates. She hasn't heard anything yet, but that it's always a possibility. We get so anxious, but try not to get our hopes up on flying early. **I just don't want any more days to go by, *any more milestones,* without us beside her.**

◆   ◆   ◆

In between carpooling children, I hear a message from Sara on the answering machine. It's Minh's birthday today, **May 3**! I dial. I know she wants to wish us a "Happy Birthday to Minh." I haven't talked to her in a while so I'm anxious for a few minutes of girl talk. I reach her but she never mentions Minh's birthday so I tell her. She says great but she's calling to tell us that we've received preliminary travel approval. *What?* This is unexpected but great news! We were initially told that we probably wouldn't be traveling until August. I then ask her to define *preliminary*. Our dossier, *that magnificent pound of paperwork*, has rapidly passed through the Vietnamese offices. All that is left is the big rubber stamp of approval from the People's Committee. We go ahead and make tentative plans to go to Vietnam. We're scheduled to arrive in Saigon May 20, pending the People's Committee *go-ahead*.

The first thing I do is call our forever-ready babysitter, my mom. She and GrandPa Tony have had their bags packed, *on stand-by status*, for months! I tell her to sit tight and I'll call with further arrangements. I call *Northwest Airlines*. They have special tickets that potential adoptive parents can purchase, called the **Special Delivery** program. They're perfect for our situation because they're tentative, changeable, with no penalty charges.

Now our wait is wracked with nervous apprehension. *What if the People's Committee denies us after all this? What if they don't approve before our scheduled flight to Vietnam? Should I go ahead and get a ticket for my mom?* She's flying up to care for Caleb, Lucas, Morgan, and Max in our absence. *Should I wait or take a chance and go ahead and purchase her ticket?* We wait, expecting to get the go-ahead each day, but hear nothing. **Sara keeps in constant contact, very supportive, *but used*. We use her to vent our frustrations. She remains an encouraging, calming sounding board.**

I decide that we can't take the chance and wait on taking care of some things, like visas. Travel visas to Vietnam take anywhere from 3 days, *if expedited*, to 2 weeks. A visa is a stamp we need in our passports giving us permission to enter and exit the country, *Vietnam*. They're obtained from the Vietnamese Embassy in Washington, D.C. I contact Zierer Visa Service to apply for mine and Jimmy's. We gather the required papers, send them and our passports off, *and wait*. Zierer assures us they'll be FedExed to us ASAP.

We also make arrangements for our children, their babysitting grandparents…It's almost the end of the school year for the children so each day is chocked full of field trips, class shows and presentations, sack lunches…Add a few orthodontic appointments and church outings to the equation and the instructions I leave for my mom resemble a novel. *She raised four children so I trust that she can handle these four. GrandPa Tony raised four, too, so they'll make a good tag team!*

I also prepare by shopping! It's a traditional Vietnamese custom *(and expected)* to offer gifts to the orphanage staff, other children at the center, and the Department of Justice officials at the "**Giving and Receiving Ceremony**." The gifts are simple, *merely tokens of appreciation*. The Binh Duong orphanage has approximately 40 children and 10 staff. *I buy extra adult gifts just in case!*

We get very nervous as the days tick by. A couple of days after Mother's Day (May 16—*two days before we're supposed to fly*), we get **THE WORD**. *Whew!* Of course in our excitement, we packed a couple of weeks ago, so that's done. Now all I have is time. I look at my children and wonder if they realize how important and special they are to me. Foreign adoption is so exciting, requires much time and patience, and is the topic of conversation for months. But, so is pregnancy and anticipating a birth. *Do they know that?* With my never-resting overactive imagination, I imagine scenarios of Jimmy and I not returning. *What if our plane crashes?* So, I sit down and write each child a letter. I tell them about my pregnancy with each one, or in Max's case, relive his domestic adoption. These letters end up being 4-5 pages each. I make sure to tell each one what I think is so special about them individually, how we anticipated their arrivals, how they kicked in my tummy, what they were like as babies, the pride we feel just knowing they're ours...*I feel much better now. I'm ready to go.*

Our visas, along with our passports, come May 17, right in time to leave the next day. My friend takes us to the airport early Friday morning (May 18) and we begin our Asian adventure.

Paddy Fields, Lotus Ponds, and Water Buffalo

Vietnam lies in the world's biggest continent, Asia. The high, forested mountains, the Annamite Range, spread over the western edge of the country separating Vietnam from Laos and Cambodia. The country is an s-shaped peninsula that borders China to the north. To the east and south is the South China Sea. Covering about 128,000 square miles, it's roughly the size of Italy.

Long and precariously thin in the middle, the country's northern and southern regions broaden into fertile delta lands—spreading out from the Red River in the north and the Mekong in the south—suggesting to many Vietnamese the familiar shape of a bamboo pole laden at each end with baskets of harvested rice. Hanoi and Ho Chi Minh City, the country's largest cities, sit in their respective northern and southern delta lands, surrounded by Vietnam's most fertile and productive rice bowls.

By the time it reaches Vietnam, the Mekong River has already covered more than 2,800 miles from its source high on the Tibetan Plateau. En route it traverses southern China, skirts Burma (Myanmar), then hugs the Laos-Thailand border before cutting down through Cambodia and into Vietnam. Silt from the Himalayan plateau is what enables this area to be so fertile and considered the country's rice bowl. It's an absolute agricultural miracle which pumps out 38% of the country's annual food crop from just 10% of its total land mass. The 9 provinces of the Delta area, beginning at Tan An, 25 miles from Ho Chi Minh City, are known as **Cuu Long** or Nine Dragons, in reference to the 9 tributaries of the Mekong spilling into the South China Sea. The number 9 is considered lucky in Vietnamese geomancy, and the Mekong Delta has certainly been lucky for its inhabitants.

Going to the Mekong offered us a fascinating glimpse into a way of life that has survived for hundreds of years. Most of it is cultivated with bright green rice paddies, fruit orchards, sugar cane fields, vegetable gardens, and the traditional fish farms. I see much diversity with the sweeping panoramas of paddies, fruit orchards and Khmer pagodas, the friendliness of the people, waterways, canals and the small tributaries. The locals live right beside the water, above in stilt houses and some even in house boats. We see river bank people at their household chores or washing. There is one woman bathing with all of her clothes on. There are children playing in the water.

The climate varies greatly from north to south. The north has four distinct seasons. Southern Vietnam has hot, humid weather throughout the year, with temperatures peaking March through May into the 90s. Southern seasonal variations are wet and dry, rather than hot and cold. The wet season lasts from May to late November, with brief daily outbursts. The dry season is from December to April.

Climate influences housing styles. Homes in the north, where the climate is cool, have walls of wood or bamboo and tile roofs. In the warm, tropical south, palm leaves and straw are common roofing materials. Throughout the country, walls made of stucco and brick can sometimes be found. In the mountains, as many as 40 family members might live in one narrow longhouse. Workers construct longhouses from palm branches, sugarcane leaves, and wooden planks. In the highland areas, homes are often built on pilings and are surrounded by trenches that provide protection from wild animals. In areas where flooding is common, homes are built on stilts. In the harbors, some people live on boats. In the city, houses and apartment buildings are only part of Vietnam's architecture. Ancient palaces crumble in the countryside. Some structures show Chinese influences. Statues and scenes from Chinese literature decorate temples. In the cities, it's also easy to see the French influence in the buildings painted yellow with detailed ironwork, shuttered windows, wide front steps, and in the wide tree-lined streets.

This country boasts a lush and varied topography. River deltas dominate the low-lying areas. The forests stay green all year-round. In the north, bamboo and hardwood trees cover the mountains and highlands. Tropical evergreens and palm trees fill rainforests in the southwestern mountains and in the lowlands. Mangrove trees hedge the coasts and wet deltas. Wet, green fields called rice paddies blanket these river deltas. The narrow central strip contains the Truong Son mountains in the west, the Central Highlands where tea and rubber trees are grown, and the Coastal Lowlands in the east where fishing and rice farming are common sources of income and subsistence.

Most of Vietnam is filled with grandiose mountains or hills. The mountains run through the country and into the sea. The mountains form hundreds of tiny islands. Water washes over 2,000 miles of coastline and meanders along thousands of canals, ditches, arroyos, and the two major rivers, altogether totaling more than 27,000 miles in length.

Canals link rivers and streams to fields. Farmers use the canals to water their rice paddies. People paddle bamboo canoes to visit neighbors or to go fishing. Other people stock their boats with rice, fish, coconuts, chickens, and vegetables to sell at floating markets. They don't even have to unload. At floating markets, the goods stay on the boats.

Water is undoubtedly the lifeblood of Vietnam. Classic images include sampans, lotus ponds and water lilies, monkey bridges, Ha Long Bay, rice paddies, water buffaloes, deserted plushy sand beaches, boat people, coolie hats…all connected with water.

We couldn't possibly take Minh to America without letting her experience the beautiful water. While at Vung Tau, she experiences the sea and sandy beaches for the first time. This was formally known as Cape Saint Jacques. It was a seaside resort in colonial times and a R-and-R center for American troops during the war. Today, there are elegant French villas in the shadow of Soviet-built concrete construction. There is also a noticeable Russian expatriate community, along with numerous North Vietnamese immigrants. The cape is the farthest extension of the Truong Mountains. It has a scenic coast road and a lighthouse. It boasts 9 miles of coastline. There are striped nautical deck chairs and broad beach umbrellas.

The Vietnamese word for "country" (**dat nuoc**) translates literally as "land-water." The legend surrounding the country's genesis involves a fight between two dragons, both so intent on obtaining a sacred pearl that their intertwined bodies fall into the South China Sea to form the sinuous land. Yet another legend relates the origins of the Viets, descendants of the family Au Co and the Dragon King Lac Long, in a symbolic marriage between land and sea.

Torrential rains and typhoons regularly flood the natural waterways, while the country's rice economy wouldn't exist without the abundance. Sampans float gently down the rivers and fishermen ply the ocean waves. Across the plains stretch endless patchworks of rice paddies, while high in the mountains thundering waterfalls create impressive spectacles.

More than 2,000 miles of coastline provide fish and other seafood. Meats such as pork, chicken, and duck are used sparingly. Vietnamese food is flavored with fresh spices and herbs. Lemongrass, chili peppers, mint, garlic, basil, and ginger add a fresh taste to many dishes. **Pho**, a hot soup made with rice noodles, beef, corn, and onion is eaten for breakfast, lunch, or dinner. **Buncha** is popular, fresh rice noodles with barbecued pork in sauce.

Early in the morning, we hear a little boy tap, tap, tapping two sticks together. This means that his mother's noodles are ready and she has set up on the sidewalk nearby. **We try to eat on the sidewalk but I just can't squat for that long like they do!** *There are women with large squid, chunky soup, greens…selling everything you can think of from their side-walk perches. Sitting on your bottom is considered lazy to the Vietnamese, as is not holding your bowl in a restaurant and scooping soup.*

Rice, the most important food in the Vietnamese diet, is served daily. Raw and cooked vegetables and tropical fruits are also common fare. Mountains of temptingly succulent fruit fill the markets of south-ern Vietnam, some of them bizarre to Western eyes and tastebuds. The Mekong Delta's island orchards send their tropical produce straight to Ho Chi Minh City. A couple of the most unusual but very delicious are the durian (**sau rieng**) and the rambutan (**chom chom**). We eat rambutans almost daily with afternoon tea.

The durian is either really hated or loved. It's as big as a football with tough thorny skin. When it's cut open, a pervasive sewer-like aroma envelopes you, but the creamy dense flesh inside is wonderful! Its strange Vietnamese name means *"one's sorrows."* They're abundant but very expensive. The rambutan is a little tough, hairy red-skinned fruit. Inside it has tender white-clear flesh whose cool sweet flavor matures during the rainy season *while we're here*. The rambutan is distantly related to the lychee.

An abundance of coconuts can be found throughout south and central Vietnam. The coconuts are large, smooth, and surprisingly *green!* The brown, hairy nut seen in our Western grocers is the small inner casing. The coconut is both multi-functional and highly nutritious. There are people everywhere selling **nuoc dua** (coconut juice). They hack off the top creating a scoop to spoon out the young, jelly-like flesh after the juice has been drunk. Coconut is also in countless candies and numerous meat dishes.

Another common food is the spring roll, known in the south as **cha gio**. There are variations of minced pork, crab, shrimps, mushrooms, beansprouts, onions, eggs, and seasoning all wrapped into a cylinder of transparent rice paper and then fried or wrapped in fresh herbs like mint. They eat the rolls by wrapping them and using chopsticks to dip them in **nuoc cham** (fish sauce).

Nuoc cham is a pungent fish sauce that's an integral part of their diet as it contains high levels of protein and replaces salt in flavoring dishes. It's served with almost every meal. The sauce is either poured over food or used for dipping. **Nuoc cham** is as common with Vietnamese meals as salt is with American dishes. It's made by fermenting specific types of fish with large quantities of salt in huge wooden vats for anywhere between 4 and 12 months. The resultant paste (**nuoc lot**) is diluted with salt water before being bottled and then placed on every Vietnamese dinner table. *As usual, there is no waste.* The fish residue left in the vats is used as a fertilizer.

They use every part of the lotus flower as well. The lotus provides edible roots, seeds, and leaves. Not just a delicacy, the flower is also symbolic as it grows up from the murky depths to the light, and as such is common in Buddhist imagery. Leaves are used to wrap sticky rice sweets; the stamens are mixed with tea to impart a special scent; and the seeds are boiled into sugary **che** or glazed and eaten as candy.

Chinese-influenced dishes can be found including **hot pot**, a cook-your-own group activity where fresh vegetables and chunks of meat and fowl are dipped into boiling broth and then consumed. The influence can also be seen in their use of woks and chopsticks. The French have left their mark, too. You'll find espresso and crusty French bread on every street corner. Foods such as asparagus and the extraordinary pastries also reflect the past French influence.

Many Vietnamese enjoy tiny meatballs, candy, noodles, eggs, or sticky rice cakes as snacks. Hawkers peddle their dish of the day from shoulder poles or hand carts. As well as the traditional meals of fish and vegetables, you can find entrees from cobra, bat, and eel. *They also have meals for people with strong stomachs.* Dog meat (**thit cay** or **thit cho**) is a delicacy where *"yellow dog"* (sandy haired varieties) is considered the tastiest. Winter is the season to eat dog meat. It's said to give extra body heat and is also supposed to remove bad luck if eaten at the end of the lunar month. Snake (**thit con ran**), like dog, is supposed to improve male virility. Dining on snake is surrounded by a ritual. If you're the guest of honor, you'll be required to eat the still-beating heart. *Give me dog any day!?!?* Another one for the strong stomach is **trung vit lon**, embryo-containing duck eggs boiled and eaten only 5 days after hatching—bill, webbed feet, feathers and all. Other exotica, very expensive, and even endangered, that may appear on menus include turtle (**rua**), pangolin (**truc**) and porcupine (**nhim**).

To finish any meal, there is a snake liquor, viperine (**ruou ran**). This is a clear liquor flavored by the corpse of a small viper curled up in the bottle. We see men all over the city hawking their *home-brew* snake wine. There's one man on a scooter with prepared wine and cages of *live poisonous vipers* strapped on the back. When someone flags him down, he kills a squirming viper and stuffs it into a waiting bottle. *On the back label it reads: "…cures rheumatism, sweat of limbs…."*

Because of the many types of land, there are many different types of plants and animals. Because of Vietnam's warm, moist weather there are tropical forests, swamp forests, exotic fruit trees, large areas of tall, sharp grasses, and coconut palms. *The coconut palm tree is an important plant. Its leaves, called fronds, are used for wrapping food and building roofs. The coconut provides milk for drinking and cooking. The meat of the coconut is also used in many dishes.* Other vital plants or crops include sugarcane, coffee, bananas, guava, papaya, strawberries, rice, tea, water lilies, potatoes, sweet potatoes, hardwood trees (teak, oak, ebony, mahogany), bamboo, pine and rubber trees, and beautiful orchids. *The exquisite orchids (**hoa lan***) *are exported worldwide.* However, many of the forests are quickly disappearing because of deforestation and poor farming techniques.

The remaining lush, tropical forests are alive with a variety of exotic animals. There are leopards, black and honey bears, monkeys, and elephants. *Elephants appear to be red because on hot days, they use their trunks to toss the cool reddish soil onto their gray hides.* These lumbering, enormous animals are used to drag logs after the trees have been cut down to create farmland. There are many snakes slithering in the forests, pythons, horse snakes, cobras…The largest is the python which can grow to 30 feet long and weigh several hundred pounds!

Seven miles from My Tho, in the southern delta, is the Dong Tam Snake Farm. This is a strange excursion for us but we're trying to experience as much as possible in these two short weeks. This farm is where pythons and cobras are raised for research into snake-based medicines. They believe snake extract can cure anything from rheumatism and headaches to insanity. Besides snakes, we see monkeys, crocodiles, deer, birds, and some strangely deformed turtles and fish. They tell us that these mutants were affected by toxic Agent Orange years ago.

Other animals that make this country their home are wild oxen, wild pigs, tapirs, barking deer, panthers, skunks, otters, and hundreds of species of birds and insects. *Silkworms are raised for the silk threads they produce to make cocoons. These threads are used to make fabric.* In the water, crocodiles, turtles, seals, and dolphins swim with brightly colored fish.

On our trip to the Saigon Zoo with the Williams, we see that the animals are in pretty dismal conditions. Of course we have a veterinarian with us so he's diagnosing as we observe. He also points out rare species that we wouldn't have been able to see in the United States. There are camels, tigers, elephants, panthers, many monkeys, birds, a big ox, some hippos, and komodo dragons. We buy pieces of bamboo and Minh feeds the elephants. She makes him do a little dance before she'll hand over the bamboo that he likes so much! There is a small walk-through aquarium that's shaped like a long, scaly lizard floating in the middle of a rather murky lily pond.

Some wild animals have been domesticated and used as work animals. Water buffaloes (**con trau**) help with plowing and hauling, and monkeys (**con khi**) are trained to climb trees and retrieve coconuts. These animals are treated as pets. In some areas, cats, dogs, ducks, and crickets are also kept as pets.

Vietnam has a cultural landscape as varied and colorful as its topography. A history of more than 1,000 years has developed a rich and varied culture, heavily spiced with remnants of other occupants. More than 79 million people live in this country. About 40% of them are younger than 15 years old. *One out of every three people is a child!* Although Vietnam is one of the most populated countries in the world, 9 out of 10 people have the same ethnic background. The ethnic Vietnamese, also called *Kinh*, are well in the majority, composing about 88% of the population. Their ancestors include long-ago Chinese settlers who made their homes in the Red River Delta. The settlers married members of other ethnic groups who moved to the area from islands in the Pacific Ocean. Over time their descendants became the ethnic Vietnamese.

There are 53 other minority ethnic groups, many of whom are hill tribes living in villages largely untouched by modern civilization. Many Chinese traders settled in Vietnam about 200 years ago. Their modern-day relatives speak Chinese and Vietnamese. Most live in Vietnam's big cities of Hanoi and Ho Chi Minh City. The Cham live in the central area where they once ruled a kingdom called Champa. Many Khmer people farm in southern Vietnam. The Tay choose mountain homes. In French, the word *"montagnard"* means "highlander." Several Tay and other ethnic groups such as the Hmong and Red Zao like life in the mountains. Together, these people are known as the Montagnards. Most Montagnards speak both Vietnamese and their own languages. Many of these people are nomads, hunters, or farmers.

About 1 in every 5 people live in a city. In the daytime, city streets fill with people walking everywhere. Walkers watch out for the motorbikes, bicycles, and **cyclos** (tricycles that carry passengers). *We try to tip generously because the economy is so bad, $1 US Dollar = $13,000 VN Dong.* At street markets, people bargain. Vendors sell delicious treats like fried bananas or meatballs. Handmade crafts are also popular. Farmers and gardeners sell fresh fruits and vegetables. At sidewalk cafes, friends chat and play cards.

The economy is still largely agrarian, with farmers, fishermen, and forestry workers accounting for 73% of the workforce and most of the population still living in villages. Life in the countryside hasn't changed for many generations. One of the special features about rural Vietnam is the village markets. In certain places, the markets float on the river. The "shops" are really boats that float along. As I mentioned earlier, people paddle smaller boats to the"shops" to buy their goods. These boats are called sampans, canoes, or **junks**.

About 80% of people live in small villages surrounded by flat, watery rice paddies. At planting time, the fields look like ponds. Soon the paddies are green with growing rice plants. Vegetable gardens and fruit trees surround houses. Many farmers raise soybeans or cotton as well as rice. When children aren't at school, they have chores. Girls help with sewing, cooking, and washing clothes. Boys carry water, help with the farming or fishing and feed the animals. **Everyone helps harvest rice!** Farmers give some of their crops to the government, which uses it to make sure people in cities have enough to eat. Farmers keep or sell the rest at open-air markets.

People who live in or near large cities dress similarly to people in large cities around the world. In rural areas, people wear more traditional clothing. Clothes are usually made of light-weight cotton for comfort in the warm, humid weather. Both men and women commonly wear wide-legged pants and loose-fitting tops. Their pants are easily rolled up when working in rice paddies. Large, conical straw hats are used for protection from the sun and rain.

For occasions such as weddings and festivals, the traditional dress of women, the **ao dai**, with its mandarin collar and long side slits is worn over free-flowing pants. The **ao dai** is usually made of hand-painted or embroidered silk. A hat called **khan dong** is worn by both children and adults. Beaded velvet slippers that curve up at the toe, called **hai**, often complete the outfit.

The people have a strong sense of family and of community and are accustomed to close human contact and far-reaching interrelationships. This may be one of the reasons why, despite centuries of occupation by foreigners, Vietnamese cultural traditions have survived.

Vietnamese people like big families. In years past, couples often had 10 or 12 children. These days, the government asks that parents have only 2 children to keep the population from growing too much, but families of 4 or 5 remain standard. Even if parents don't have a lot of children, extended families—which include grandparents, cousins, aunts and uncles—like to live together. Children are supposed to respect and obey their parents and other adults. Older people are considered wise and experienced. Children might help their parents by shopping, cooking, cleaning, and caring for the youngest and oldest family members.

Some large families in rural areas use numbers as given names. More often, families give names that reflect their hopes for their children. We met a girl named *Nguyen Hoa*. **Hoa** is her true name and it means *"flower."* Her name is a wish that she grow as lovely as a flower. There was a boy, **Toan**, which means *"fulfillment."*

In the past, parents picked whom their children would marry. Today, most people choose their own spouses. To get engaged, a man visits a woman's house to ask her father for permission to marry her. Then the families of the husband and wife exchange gifts of cake, nuts, and teas. On their wedding day, brides and grooms may wear traditional clothes. *As part of the ceremony, each eats a piece of ginger root dipped in salt. The harsh taste reminds them of challenges they might face together.* Then everyone goes to the groom's house for a huge feast. More prosperous families might *foot the bill* for an elaborate reception in a fancy hotel or favorite restaurant. *At the Rex, we see two wedding feasts with hundreds of attendees at each party.*

Due to the high birthrate, many children reach school age each year. As a result, schools are overcrowded. To keep the class sizes down, one group of children attend school from early morning until midday. A second group takes classes in the afternoon. Education is free and highly valued. The school system is made up of elementary, middle, and highschool. School week begins Monday and ends Saturday. The school year lasts from September until May, *much like ours.* Children ages 6 to 11 attend primary school. Some attend secondary school (highschool) but most leave school to work. Although education is respected, some children, especially in the rural areas, can't attend because they must work to help provide for their family's basic needs.

Children are expected to take school very seriously and perform well. Many schools have no playground equipment or extracurricular activities. Teachers often begin each class with an oral exam and call upon students to stand and respond to questions. At the end of the week, students stand and tell the teacher what they've learned. In addition to Reading, Math, Science, and Social Studies, students are taught traditional manners and customs. Students don't receive letter grades. Instead, students are ranked first, second, third, and so on. Parents are regularly informed of their child's rank. At the end of the school year top students may be rewarded with gifts of school supplies.

In schools and elsewhere, you'll hear Vietnamese of course. In the cities, you can also hear people speaking Chinese, Russian, and English. If you go to the smaller villages, you'll hear people speaking ancient languages just as their relatives did hundreds of years ago.

Speaking Vietnamese is like singing a song. There are high tones and low tones, changing tones, and flat tones. A word's meaning is determined by the pitch at which you deliver it. Six tones are used. Depending upon its tone, the word "**ba**" can mean *three, grandmother, poisoned food, waste, aunt,* or *any.* If you say the word "**ma**" in a high tone, you mean *mother.* In a flat tone, the word means *ghost.* So, though not complex structurally, the language is tonal and therefore difficult for many Westerners to master. There are three main dialects—northern, central, and southern—used and although similar, *pronunciation can be so wildly variant that some locals have trouble understanding each other.*

Hundreds of years ago, people used characters (symbols) to write Vietnamese. These days, Vietnamese is written with the same alphabet used to write English. In most words, each syllable is written separately, so the Vietnamese write Vietnam as "Viet Nam." Small lines or other symbols above or next to the letters indicate their tone. The Vietnamese call this form of writing **quoc ngu**. It's the modern official writing system used but the old system of using characters is preferred for fancy signs and important documents, such as government or religious papers.

The government doesn't encourage religions but more than half practice *Buddhism*. We hardly see any observance to Communism at all, other than the prevalence of state-owned entities. About 70% are Buddhists, *mainly Mahayana*. Followers of Buddhism believe in a cycle of life and rebirth, in peace, and in cooperation. Most Buddhist monks and nuns live, study, and work in pagodas. Fancy carving, painted wood, and statues of Buddha make the pagodas and temples beautiful.

There are also a small percentage of *Confucianists*. This religion teaches people to respect and obey parents, teachers, and government leaders. Some are *Taoists*. They try to live in harmony with nature. The Vietnamese Taoists believe in many gods and spirits, such as the Jade Emperor, who rules heaven.

When visiting the Emperor Jade Pagoda, we see large turtles in the pond on the grounds. This pagoda, **Phuoc Hai**, *is sometimes fittingly called the "tortoise pagoda." This pagoda too is filled with smoky incense and contains fantastic carved figurines. It's kind of spooky! A statue of the Jade Emperor lords over the main hall's central altar. This statue monitors entry into Heaven and his two keepers of Heaven—one holding a lamp to light the way for the virtuous, the other wielding an ominous looking ax—flank his sides. I find myself praying silently. I've been doing that a lot recently. There's a statue of Kim Hua, the goddess of fertility. I steer clear of that idol, with my five children and all!?!? Countless women are bowed to the floor in front of her, praying for children. It gets almost sinister when we walk into a chamber and see* **Thanh Hoang**, *the Ruler of Hell, with his red horse. This room is eerily filled with wood panels that represent the 1,000 torments of Hell. If this doesn't make us act right, nothing will.*

Many people combine Buddhist, Confucian and Taoist beliefs. There are minuscule pockets of practicing Islamic. Europeans brought Christianity to Vietnam and these days some people are Roman Catholic Christians.

*The Notre Dame Cathedral (**Nha Tho Duc Ba**) is right downtown amid the businesses. The cathedral was built in 1880 on the site of the Citadel's arsenal. It has a Neo-Romanesque red-brick facade, framed by 2 square 131-foot towers. The power and grace of it is stunning. I think I'm so enchanted by it because of it being such a formidable structure nestled in a seemingly Communist country. They used bricks from Marseilles and stained-glass windows from Chartres.*

Still others are *Animists*, people that believe in gods of nature. Vietnamese have a lot of respect for their ancestors. Many houses have small altars covered with photos and other symbols of loved ones who have died. At certain times of year, they leave out food and drink for their ancestors' ghosts.

*While in Vung Tau on the South China Sea, we go to the Whale Temple (**Lang Ca Dng**). Vung Tau fishermen regard the mammal as their patron god and some of the whale bones displayed behind the altar are centuries old. It should be preserved in a Smithsonian-type institution but* *instead they have Christmas lights around and in the display case holding the bones, twinkling and cheerily gaudy.*

There are also followers of the unique Vietnamese religion *Cao Daism*, an interesting combination of the major world faiths. Ngo Van Chieu formed the Cao Dai religion in the 1920s, following a revelation of "the way" in a vivid dream. In 1926, one of his followers, Le Van Trung, deserted with 20,000 loyal converts, crowned himself Pontiff and built the Cao Dai temple at Tay Ninh. Seven years later, he was deposed for embezzling the temple funds. By 1939, there were more than 4 million Cao Dais, and by the mid-1950s, one in 8 South Vietnamese was a Cao Dai. After WWII, the followers dabbled in politics, formed private armies, shifts in support, a breakaway Buddhist sect…until President Ngo Dinh Diem outlawed both sects in 1955. Today, authorities won't "allow" a new Pontiff to be appointed but over 2 million Vietnamese still follow the Cao Dai way. Sermons by planchette, originally seances held to contact people like Sun Yat Son and Victor Hugo, are no longer practiced. Cao Daism seeks to create the ultimate religion by fusing Buddhist, Taoist, Confucionist, and Catholic beliefs into a synthesis of its own.

I feel like I've stepped into a cult. In a corner of the temple is a bizarre acrobatic statue depicting Jesus, Lao Tse, Confucius, and Buddha standing on each other's shoulders!?!? This is unbelievable! The **Cao Dai Holy See,** as it's called, is a huge fantasy cathedral. It's strange, with dragons and snakes in technicolor. There are pink pillars entwined by green dragons and neon pink lotus blossoms. The temple has 8 stages in a progression leading to an altar and a huge orb-like eye. The altar groans under the weight of assorted vases, fruit, paintings, and slender statues of storks…yes pink flamingo lawn decoration type birds!?!? Each stage represents a step to heaven. The papal chair stands at the head of the chamber, its arms carved into dragons. Below it are six more chairs, three with eagle arms and three with lion detailing for the cardinals. Dominating the chamber and guarded by 8 scary silver dragons, a vast egg-blue sphere speckled with stars, rests on a polished eight-sided dais. The "Divine Eye" peers through clouds painted on the front. There are more glittery stars and fluffy clouds on the sky-blue ceiling, as well as statues of resting lions and turtles. Throughout the temple are gaudy curtains and pastel-colored stucco work. Everywhere is the Cao Daist symbol, a triangle enveloping a "holy eye."

Women enter on the left and men on the right. All "worshipers," including us, remove shoes and leave them outside. We're led silently up to a balcony to watch the noon service. We are to be silent, not distracting…A band with ancient instruments plays in the balcony. Most worshipers dress in white robes and turbans. Some wear yellow, blue, and red. I'm not sure of the significance. Priests don red robes and square hats emblazoned with the "Divine Eye." Worshipers' heads nod in time to the clanging of a gong.

Then a haunting, measured chanting begins and doesn't end for 45 minutes. I find myself silently praying…the red robes, the chanting…all a little bewildering! As prayers and "hymns" continue, incense, flowers, alcohol, and tea are offered up to the "Supreme Being."

Minh starts humming with the followers and even attempts to sing along. We rapidly decide that it's time for us to find an exit. Cao Dais with armbands wander about and answer theological questions, mostly by rote, and make sure all followers are correctly participating. Within the compound are a vast array of related colorful structures. It's a city within a city. Neighboring villages are all Cao Daist and followers can be spotted in their white robes.

Most music is played during religious rituals and for the theater. They bang drums, gongs, and cymbals. The bamboo flute and Chinese oboe are part of Vietnamese orchestras. A dried gourd, stick, and a long copper wire make an instrument called a **dan ball**. Some bang out tunes on the stone xylophone, called a **to rung**. Different sized stones are chosen for the sounds they make when struck. The music, using string and woodwind instruments, bamboo or the stone xylophone, metal gongs, is delicate, distinctive, and appealing.

The binding element to all Vietnamese traditional performing arts is music, and particularly singing (**hat**) which is a natural extension to an already musical language. Ancient Vietnamese art forms remain today, like water puppetry, where wooden hand puppets actually dance across water, and **cheo**, traditional folk opera. Young people tend to listen to pop music.

Vietnam has a long tradition of handmade goods. There's an emerging interest in fine arts, with countless galleries in almost every major city and an emphasis in traditional techniques such as lacquer, silk paintings, and wood blocking. Ceramics (pottery) is also a popular art form.

The exquisite lacquerware (**son mai**) is embellished with intricate inlays of mother-of-pearl. Artists shape pieces of wood into boxes, vases, and furniture. They decorate the wood using designs of inlaid material, then apply many coats of lacquer. Each layer of this clear, glossy liquid takes 7 days to dry.

Block printing, a method of making patterned cloth and paper, is ancient but still popular. Workers carve patterns, flowers, or scenes from daily life onto flat blocks of wood. They then ink the block before pressing it onto paper or cloth. The ink leaves a beautiful design.

The importance of weaving can be seen in everyday Vietnamese life. Weaving is used in thatched roofs, decorative wall hangings, boats, straw mats, baskets, and even hats. The highland tribes weave their own cloth on handmade looms, Each tribe creates its own distinctive designs using small, repeated patterns enhanced with silver and beads.

In Ho Chi Minh City, there are beautiful paintings on rice paper, elaborate silk **ao dais**, lacquerware, embroidered cloth, exceptional greeting/note cards that reveal typical Vietnamese scenes hand-painted onto silk. There is also handmade jewelry, woven baskets, creative and enduring tapestries, and many books.

Literature has existed since the forming of the nation in folklore, proverbs and idioms singular to each village and ethnic group and passed down from century to century. Many of the old tales have been translated and printed in books that can be easily found in foreign-language bookstores. They have a multitude of books revealing Vietnam's long and tumultuous history.

*We want to learn more and see more of Vietnam generations ago so we take a cab to the History Museum, **Bao Tang Lich Su Viet Nam**. The Museum consists of 2 main parts. The first displays the history of Vietnam beginning some 300,000 years ago until the time which preceded the birth of the Communist Party. It takes us through the very primitive period, the many dynasties through the centuries up until the Nguyen dynasty (19th-middle of 20th century). It's simply fascinating to be able to see, and in some instances, touch an artifact that has been on this earth for centuries. The second part displays a number of special subjects bearing the characteristics of the South including the Oc Eo culture (1st-6th century), art of the*

Mekong (7th-13th century), Cham sculpture and other artifacts. There's a bizarre statue of Kuan Yin with one thousand eyes and one thousand arms carved in 1656.

There's a whole courtyard with nothing but cannons and even a female corpse unearthed when construction workers broke ground for a new housing project. What I find most interesting is the wing dedicated to ethnic minorities of the South, including photographs, costumes, and household implements.

Vietnam's history reveals a pattern of violent confrontations and clashes between dynasties and kingdoms seeking to expand their territory. China's *Han* Dynasty was the dominating force for more than 1,000 years. China invaded and conquered the area around the Red River Delta in the second century B.C. and maintained a presence until they were finally forced out in A.D. 938. Nearly 600 years later, French and Portuguese traders had arrived in Vietnam. By 1883 France had control. They built railroads and government buildings. This foreign power harshly treated and heavily taxed the Vietnamese.

The next 100 years saw Colonialism give way to war, first with the French, then with the Americans.

War broke out in 1945 after the Vietnamese declared independence from France. Vietnam won in 1954. The Vietnamese then couldn't agree on what kind of government to have. North and South Vietnam were soon at war, both wanting to rule the other. They fought for years. Eventually, North Vietnam won the war. During the fighting, millions died and many parts of the country were destroyed.

We're taken to see the Cu Chi Tunnels built in the 1940s, when fighters against the French army dug a network of tunnels for hiding themselves and ammunition. The network was expanded during the 1960s for the Viet Cong insurgents and then during the American War. This edifying structure with an elaborate 250km of tunnels branched out like a cobweb spread below ground, from Cambodia into the heart of South Vietnam. The tunnel network zigzags underground from the main path to a multitude of short and long ramifications. There were venues with mouths having access to the Saigon River. These mouths allowed the hiding people to cross the river to Ben Cat Base Zone (in Binh Duong Province) when the situation was critical. By 1965, tunnels criss-crossed Cu Chi and surrounding areas. Just across the Saigon River was the notorious guerilla power base known as the Iron Triangle, making it possible for the VC guerrilla in the area to link up with each other and to infiltrate Saigon at will. One section daringly ran underneath the American Cu Chi Army Base. This complex was at times home to almost 10,000 Viet Cong.

Our personal tour starts in a classroom with a wall chart showing the cross-section of tunnels. From there, we head into the bush. The guide points out tiny trap doors used long ago. The Vietnamese are small so the doors are teeny. They have no trouble slipping right in. Jimmy tries but only makes it up to his thighs. During the war, GIs would lob down gas or grenades trying to flush out the VC. They used small-framed die-hard soldiers to go down themselves for underground raids. These small Americans were called tunnel rats. Another tactic involved dropping leaflets and broadcasting bulletins that played on the fighters' fears and loneliness. The Napalm/Agent Orange killed all vegetation so the jungle is full of young trees. They have set pretend booby traps throughout the area. I don't see a string and end up tripping a wire. It sets off a firecracker. It really scares me! Jimmy is very tense, finding this all unnerving to say the least. There are carcasses of helicopters and tanks, self-manufactured mines, traps...

The tunnels could be as small as 80cm wide and 80 cm high, sometimes 4 levels deep. Vent shafts to disperse smoke and aromas from underground ovens were camouflaged by thick grass and termites' nests. The tunnels were foul-smelling and so hot that by afternoon inhabitants had to lie on the floor in order to get enough oxygen. Darkness was absolute and some long-term dwellers suffered temporary blindness when they emerged into the light. Cu Chi subsequently became the most densely bombed area within Vietnam and suffered heavy defoliation during the 60s when the Americans, fed up with being ambushed, set about bombing the area out of existence.

The tunnels sheltered troops, held schools, hospitals, kitchens and stores, even multi-colored quarters. Some tunnels are enlarged for foreigners to get a feel of how the VC lived. We drop to our hands and knees, squeeze underground, for an insight... They take Jimmy and I down into a tunnel that leads to a small kitchen with a wood oven and long, narrow tables. We eat tapioca root dipped in crushed peanuts and hot tea, often the only food source available to tunnel dwellers. It feels like a sauna! Even though the tunnels have been widened to allow passage for the fuller frame of Westerners, it's still a dark, sweaty, claustrophobic experience!

In 1976, Vietnam was finally one independent country again, but at a terrible cost. The nation united under a Communist government. Rather than enjoying this newfound peace, Vietnam invaded Cambodia after border skirmishes in 1978. China, friend of Cambodia, then invaded Vietnam in 1979.

In the mid 1980s, the country began moving toward **doi moi**, a free-market policy. It withdrew its army from Cambodia in 1989 to further ingratiate itself with the international community. As the

1990s began, Vietnam began opening to the world. It further reorganized its economy toward a market-oriented model, sought diplomatic relations, and in 1991 signed a peace agreement with Cambodia. In 1994, America capitulated and lifted its long-standing trade embargo against Vietnam, and the two countries established diplomatic relations in 1995. Vietnam also joined ASEAN (Association of Southeast Asia Nations).

Because of war, Vietnam has a lot of problems. Most of the country has not been rebuilt. Many of the factories and businesses were destroyed. Many Vietnamese people have left hoping to make a better life somewhere else. The Vietnamese are proud people, however, and most have stayed in their homeland. Economic momentum is leaving much of the rural population out in the cold. Vietnam ranks with Bangladesh as one of the world's poorest nations with a per capita income of US$280. Top wage earners make up to 40 times as much as the lowest. Government officials, teachers, and doctors earn a mere US$50 per month, an income shortfall that generates corrupt practices among the former and moonlighting among the professionals.

While its political system is still dominated by the Communist Party, the Vietnamese government has demonstrated flexibility and encouraged initiative in its relationships with other countries. This so-called Communist state is in fact, relentlessly Capitalist. The child hawkers, "tour guides," and cyclo drivers can be extraordinarily persistent, following you for blocks, grabbing your arm, hounding you at temples and restaurants. With liberalizing foreign investment loans and relaxing visa regulations, Vietnam today is flourishing somewhat. It has become the world's third largest rice exporter. Its per capita income increases steadily each year, though mammoth pockets of extreme poverty still remain.

The contrasts can be easily seen in the large cities. Vietnam's two largest cities are at opposite ends of the country. The capital, Hanoi, is *the administrative heart* in the north, while the most populated city is in the south, Ho Chi Minh City, *the country's commercial pulse.* Ho Chi Minh City is in an economic revival, although it's still bursting with the unfortunate that go without food, housing, and jobs. Amid the changes, construction everywhere, the population of over 6 million go about their daily routines. Ho Chi Minh City is full of vitality and promise, *a flurry of activity.* But among the hustle and bustle, the teens in designer jeans chatting on mobile phones and people frequenting karoke bars, are pockets of tranquility and tradition in the Buddhist pagodas hidden around the city, the schoolgirls clad in white traditional silk **ao dai**, and the altars to the ancestors in every shop and house.

We spend the majority of our time in and around Ho Chi Minh City. This southern city was founded in the 18th century. It was settled by Civil War refugees from North Vietnam and Chinese merchants. The city was the capital of the Republic of South Vietnam in 1954 but fell to the North Vietnamese forces on 30 April 1975. It was renamed Ho Chi Minh City the following year, yet it's still known by its former name, **Saigon**, to the majority of its inhabitants and visitors.

Lying at the base of the s-shaped country, Ho Chi Minh City is bordered by the Saigon River to the east and a flat plain stretching as far as Phnom Penh in Cambodia to the west. Some 62 miles southwest, the Mekong Delta widens to the pounding waves of the South China Sea.

The city is crowded, exciting, historic, and boasts wildly busy streets. Ho Chi Minh City is divided into districts. District 1 borders the Saigon River. This is the business, cultural, more touristy area.

The Saigon Opera House (Ho Chi Minh Municipal Theater) is right beside our hotel, in the cultural district. It was built at the turn of the century and renovated in the 1940s. It is three stories and houses 1,800 seats. It hosts native and international opera troupes, orchestras, and ballets. It was forever busy during our short stay.

The Reunification Palace (Hoi Truong Thong Nhat) is also in District 1. This was the site of the Norodom Palace, a colonial mansion erected in 1971 to house the governor-general of Indochina. With the French departure in 1954, President Ngo Dinh Diem commandeered this extravagant monument as his Presidential Palace, but after sustaining extensive damage in a February 1962 assassination attempt by 2 disaffected Southern pilots, the place was condemned and pulled down. The newly built building was labeled the Independent Palace upon completion in 1966, only to be retitled the more politically correct Reunification Hall when the South fell in 1975. The reversion to "palace" was made for tourist appeal. Architect, Ngo Viet Thu, designed details from the chandeliers down to the carpets. It's like we go back in time. The furniture, decor in general, all sixties/ early seventies. What is interesting is the War Command Room with its huge maps and old communication equipment.

District 3 is residential with some fine old villas and gardens. *The War Crimes Museum and Emperor Jade Pagoda are in District 3.* To the far west is District 5, the Chinese quarter of Cholon.

The ethnic Chinese, or **Hoa**, first began to settle here around the turn of the 19th century. Many came from existing enclaves in My Tho and Bien Hoa. The area soon became the largest Hoa community in the country, still is with over half a million. It's probably the largest Chinatown in the world. Cholon is a fascinating maze of temples, restaurants, jade ornaments, and medicine shops. The name **Cholon** means "big market."

We go to the **Binh Tay** market in Cholon one day. It's very crowded, cyclo drivers clogging the front entrance. The building is multi-tiered with mustard-colored roofs and statues of serpentine dragons "standing guard." This is one of the most fascinating places we've visited yet! There are buckets of eels, clutches of live frogs tied together at the legs, heaps of pig ears and snouts, baskets wedged full of hens, even geese and ducks tied together, dried fish, and pottery piled up to the rafters. The aroma is a strong conflicting mixture of jasmine and incense. The colors of the vegetables are endless and the fruits are ripe and fresh. There are people hawking medicinal herbs like cinnamon bark and star anise, as well as strange forms of noodles and dried mushrooms.

While in Cholon, we visit what they call a typical Chinese pagoda, **Thien Hau Temple**. *It's beautiful, with a carved gold-painted wooden boat hanging over the entrance. There are mysterious, large spirals hanging from the ceiling. Inside them are week-long incense coils. It's as smoky as any bar I've strolled into, burning incense filling the air. People are praying for healthy children, money, the desires of their heart.*

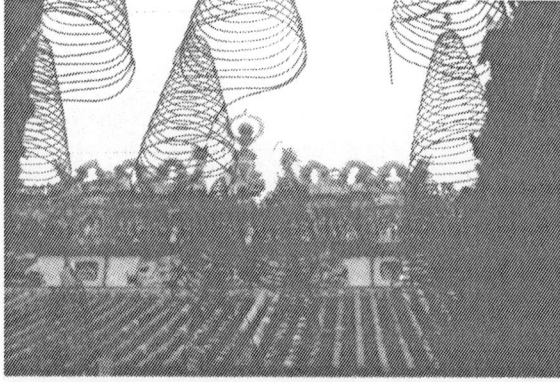

South of the canals is the less prosperous and often impoverished Districts 4 and 8. We never go there even though I want to. It's too dangerous, especially when carrying a 2 year-old.

Daily Journal Entries of our Southeast Asian Adventure

Saturday, May 19

We arrive in Bangkok, Thailand around 11PM. At the airport, we exchange some of our dollars for **Thai Baht** since American money isn't readily accepted here. We rent a taxi (a Mercedes) to our hotel, the Rama Gardens. *The driver runs out of gas on the way, but he conveniently has a bottle of gas in his trunk.* He fills it up and we're on our way. We check in around midnight and go downstairs to have a look around. **We're too excited to sleep!** We order wine and shrimp cocktail at a little lounge in the hotel. Huge, raw shrimp are lying on a cut papaya. We learn that Thais eat most seafood raw, *right out of the water.* Rock songs waft in from the nearby lounge, *karoke bar.* We watch them sing and party for a while before going up to bed.

It's a nice room but we can't figure out how to make any power (lights, air condition…) come on. *I remember one of my friends had the same problem on a trip to India.* After a thorough search, we see a slot by the door that conveniently holds our room key, and *the answer* to the power. Right outside our window are beautiful , climbing, thick flowers and vines with sharp, treacherous thorns, *for security.*

Sunday, May 20

We get up real early and go down for breakfast. I have an omelette with toast and yogurt. Jimmy tries the traditional Thai meats, cheeses, frothy soup and rice. *The hotel grounds are exquisite! There are colorful, lush flowers and plants everywhere!* Ornate, small bridges overlook lily ponds and shocking pink flowers. The Rama Gardens has two pools and a big sports complex. We meet our hired driver and guide in the lobby around 10AM, whole day for US$20. **It's so hot!** *I already have that sheen on my face that will undoubtedly remain until I get back to Pennsylvania.* Our guide's name is Nancy, she says "like Nancy Reagan." Our driver doesn't talk much.

Bangkok is huge, 10 million people. It's very clean and surprisingly modern-looking. Nancy has 2 children. She says "Bangkok is a good place to make money, not to live." *There's a lot of pollution and cars everywhere!* They do have a good public transportation system but most choose not to take advantage of it. There are also countless *tuk-tuks* (3-wheeled open-air taxis). *They're called tuk-tuks because that's the sound they make when puttering down the streets.*

We pass the Thewes Flower Market (**Ta-laat Tay-wait**). It opens daily around 2AM. *There are beautiful cut and potted flowers and plants.* We don't go in but pass the Grand Palace. Since 1946, the Thai royal family has lived in another palace, **Chitrlada**, in the northern area of Bangkok. The Grand Palace is still used for state ceremonies. Since Rama I's reign, each new monarch has slept in the majestic bedchamber the first night after his coronation. In the courtyard, there are gold-knobbed red poles. *Nancy explains that the royal elephants were once tethered there.*

We stop at the colossal **Phra Pathom Chedi**. This is supposed to be the world's tallest Buddhist stupa. Originally dating to 300 B.C. the chedi was raised to its present height of 420 feet by King Mongkut in 1860. Its base is full of frangipani trees. People are buying incense, candles, *even lotus buds* to take to the Buddha and make a wish or pray.

The Marble Wat (**Wat Benchamabophit**) is where we see an unusual alms-giving ritual. The monks wait silently in the tree-shaded street in front of the temple and the faithful take them food. The temple was made from Italian Carrara marble in 1911, *simply breath-taking!* The colorful decorations that adorn the white marble are ceramic.

There are 53 Buddhist images represented here. These statues are supposed to show the different ways Buddha has been portrayed throughout history in South and Southeast Asia. Also inside are elaborate stained-glass windows depicting angels, *not something we expect to see in a Thai temple.*

Wat Po (Temple of the Reclining Buddha) is our next stop. This temple predates the birth of Bangkok by a century. Here lies the 107 feet reclining Buddha. On the enormous feet are 108 signs (or **laksana**) by which a Buddha can be recognized, rendering intricate mother-of-pearl patterns. Wat Po is highly regarded as a center of traditional medicine. In the courtyard, we step into the School of Traditional Thai Massage. *It looks painful!*

Temples also serve as animal asylums. When people have a litter of puppies they don't want, they take them to the Wat where they'll eat the monks' leftovers. *People drop off cats, elephants…*Before heading back to the hotel, we turn our gaze on the solid gold Buddha weighing 51/2 tons at the **Wat Trimit.**

We get back to the hotel just in time to catch a taxi to the airport. Somehow we get bumped up to First Class! We stay in the lounge and eat cake and sandwiches, wine…The flight to Saigon, or the proper name, *Ho Chi Minh City*, is very enchanting! They pamper us and ply us with champagne. We arrive in Saigon around 10PM. We only have to wait a few minutes before our Holt facilitator rushes up to introduce herself and gets us a taxi. We are taken to the Rex Hotel, *our home for the next couple of weeks.*

On the roof terrace is a huge crown full of sparkly lights, the hotel's emblem. We are awed by all of the lights, glitz, and chaos when we enter the lobby. The hotel is obviously in a fabulous downtown location, in the heart of the city. In front of the entrance is a small courtyard with a beautiful fountain and a lively carnival atmosphere. It appears to be a magnet for vendors, courting couples, and beggars.

The Rex Hotel was built in 1960. It has only operated as a hotel since 1976. It started out as a garage for the Renaults and Peugeots of the city's French community. During the 1960s (1962-1970), *during the war*, it was home to American officers, the U.S. Information

Agency, and some say the CIA. It also hosted regular press briefing sessions that came to be known by jaded members of the press as the "Five O'Clock Follies."

After massive renovations, the Rex opened as the government hotel it is today. *The rooms are laden with bamboo detailing on the ceilings, the mirror, chairs, everywhere! The beds are covered with silk bedspreads and the lampshades are big royal "crowns." The neatest amenity are the bright-colored, silk his and hers kimonos. There are other quirky tidbits and decorations throughout, right down to the beaded curtains, complementary slippers, and the ever-necessary umbrella!* The Rex is home to a popular rooftop restaurant and bar with a panoramic Saigon view, pool, health club, and three restaurants.

Monday, May 21

I'm awake! It's 4AM! I'm all ready, just sitting in a chair, thinking and waiting. ***We're getting our little girl today!*** I have daily, *sometimes minutely*, prayed for her. I'm very excited, of course, but also nervous. The end to a long process is culminating at a nearby orphanage in just a few hours.

Neither one of us can eat much breakfast. We decide to walk around, to calm our nerves before meeting Nguyen Thi Lan Huong (our Holt facilitator) and the driver in the lobby. It takes about an hour for us to get to the orphanage in the Binh Duong Province. I can see why a driver is more or less required. If there are any traffic rules used, for the life of me, I don't see them or understand them. ***Binh Duong*** *is located in southern Vietnam. It's surrounded by Binh Phuoc to the north, Tay Ninh to the west, Dong Nai to the east, and Ho Chi Minh City to the south.*

We pull up at the orphanage in Binh Duong and are greeted by the regional director, Le Binh. We've heard a lot about him from the correspondence we've received. There are little ones walking around, peeking out at us. We sit in Le Binh's office while he goes over our schedule, upcoming paperwork requirements, Minh's usual daily/feeding schedule, etc. *There's a little boy hanging on the bars outside of Binh's office window, smiling at us.* Le Binh gives us a precious gift, a photo album that the staff has created. It details Minh's life at the orphanage starting from the first day she arrives as a 3-month-old up until the photo they take the day before. *Priceless!*

A few minutes later, in walks our angel, *Gracie Minh*, known here as Pham Tam Minh.

I look over at Jimmy and he's just grinning, silent. *I don't think my heart beats for a long while. I just look at Minh. She's so much smaller than I thought for some reason.* Like any new parent, we count her *ten perfect fingers and ten diminutive toes.* Although I've had ample time to get accustomed to her physical setbacks, I find my eyes immediately drawn to her mouth. *I pray that we haven't gotten in over our heads, that we can indeed get her the medical treatments she needs.*

Her eyes are enchanting, just like in her pictures that I've treasured for months. Her downy, dusky hair is short and thin in places. She has on thin, tiny white panties, an old yellow tanktop, a big drool bib, and flashy, glittery purple suede shoes. She shuffles around and stands in front of us, staring. *She knows us—I feel it!* I want to hug her close so bad but she seems skittish. I put my arm out to her and she runs to Le Binh. He speaks to her in Vietnamese and she nods. She takes a little comb out of his pocket and he combs her hair with it. Jimmy and I give her a little adjustment time.

Minh is holding a photo book, full of photos of us, our kids and her siblings, our house, her bedroom in America…The orphanage director, a nice lady, asks her *"Where is your ma ma?"* She looks at her photo book. They point to me in a photo and then to me. They ask her again and she points to me. They ask her *"Where is your pa pa?"* She looks at the photos and she points right to Jimmy. *They've tried to prepare her for her new life with us.*

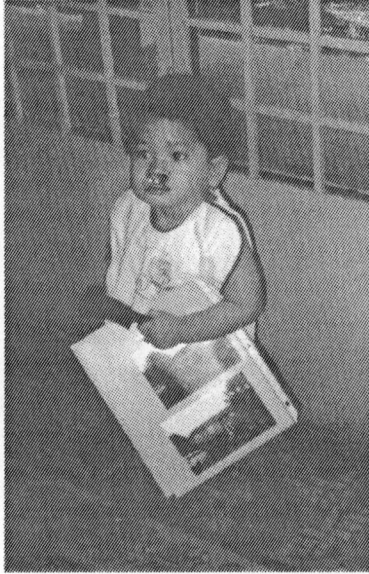

I get out some stickers which seem to fascinate her. She comes right over and we sit down to play on the floor with those, some crayons and paper. She's slowly warming up to us. Of course we have stickers all over our hands and cheeks. *I can't believe that we're actually here making preparations to bring her home. Even though she's a little shy with us, she does seem to know us, like she's been waiting just for us to come to her.* I sit her in my lap finally and she savors all the attention. The staff is very loving, encouraging, and patient with her. *Actually, I think she has Le Binh wrapped around her little finger.*

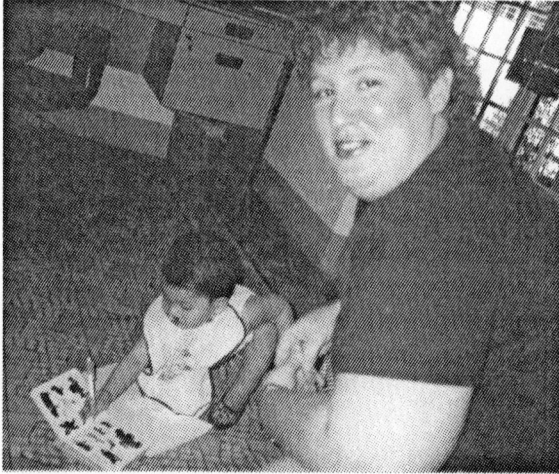

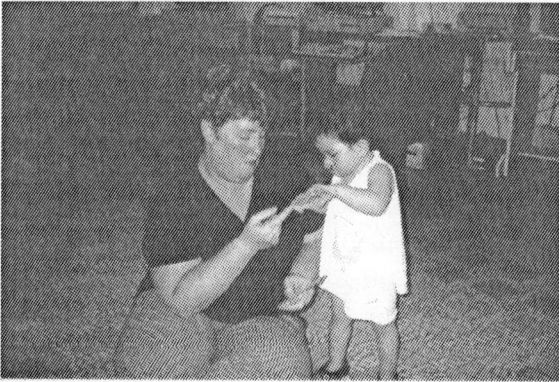

The orphanage director comes in and tells us that the judge is waiting for us now at the Department of Justice. He came back after starting out on a trip to Hanoi, just for us, so we better hurry. We get in the
van. The director sits in the back so Minh can't see her. Le Binh leads
the way on his scooter. Minh looks out the window, at us, taking in the
sights, smells, and sounds.

It's a short trip. We walk in and the sea of people literally part for
us. They're gawking, whispering, even pointing at Minh. She stares
back with a distant look in her eyes. The officials are preparing for the

"Giving and Receiving Ceremony" as we walk in. Jimmy and I hold Minh. Le Binh is there as translator. The judge stands before us and asks if we'll always love her and make her a part of our family. He asks if we can "fix" her. He asks if we'll tell her of her heritage and maybe one day bring her back to see her beginnings. He explains that the Vietnamese government requires that we send a letter detailing her progress, information about her life, and 10 photos every year until she reaches 18 years of age. We anxiously agree to all stipulations and requests. We sign several documents, as do the judge and participating justice officials. We give all officials gifts of appreciation, Coleman flashlight and pen sets. They approve. We get a couple of slaps on the back and we depart for Immigration.

We file for her passport. The official asks to speak *only to the men.* The director, Minh, and I are asked to wait outside, *so we do.* While outside, the director asks how I can handle all of my children. She says she feels sorry for me having to take care of Minh. I tell her that in America, she'll have surgeries, learn to talk…have a normal life. That's nothing to feel sorry about. We *chose* Minh, from many different children. **We're happy!** The paperwork is taken care of pretty fast and we head back to the orphanage.

Minh is a little confused. She walks out to the room with the rest of the children (orphans) then wanders back in to look at us. Le Binh gives us a tour of the compound. The orphanage isn't gated but has a blue and white entrance. There's some rudimentary concrete playground equipment in the front. We don't see any children playing on it. Binh has a small room there where he lives. There are a couple of offices, a baby room, and a room for the older children. The children have wooden beds with bamboo-woven mats to lie on and no covers. The infant/toddler beds are large, wooden, and usually house 1-3 children. All floors are concrete. *The children are cute, bowing their traditional greeting.* One little boy, around 4 years old, follows us everywhere, chirping and grunting. He can't speak. Even when we're in the office he climbs on something to peer in the windows. The other half of the compound consists of open rooms with wooden beds, and the bamboo mats, but occupied by the very elderly, *a nursing home*. Strange!

The courtyard between the two buildings is dirt, no grass. They have clothes drying on lines. We come up on a concrete foundation, wooden bunk beds, with a tarp-like roof. Le Binh explains that this is where the older boys sleep and play.

Down a narrow path is a building that houses a tiny *kitchen*. There's an older model stove and a woman cooking on a wok for 50 people. On the floor is a kale soup, cooling in a big pot. There's a kitchen worker squatting, filling lunch trays. Outside are bowls of fruit, lettuce, *all part of the kitchen*. Right across from the kitchen are two heavy-padded doors with small barred windows. Le Binh explains that those are "mental problems." *There's a teen looking out at us.*

The director says it's now time to give out the presents we brought for the children, and staff. We give the staff *Bath and Body* goodies which they seem to like. The men get *Coleman* pharaphanelia. We take a big bag full of matchbox cars, baby dolls, puzzles, beannie babies…to the biggest room. The children all crowd around and wait. Le Binh dumps the bag of toys on the floor and the children act like a pinata has just burst open. They scramble, trying to grab their fair share. *Even Minh is sitting on the floor with her legs spread out, raking toy cars in with her legs and arms.*

We take a few toys to the baby room, Minh's *home* since she was 3 months old. We remove our shoes as we enter as instructed. The babies crawl and play on the floor so they try to keep it as clean as possible. These little ones are loving the special attention! Jimmy and I sit on the floor with them and play with the baby toys we brought. There are two tiny babies. The rest are young toddlers. *Minh feels special now. She walks around with us as we play with the children and give out presents.* As we're leaving, a cute little boy with a lot of hair spiked up screams and cries, trying to go with us. *It's rare that anyone comes and sits on the floor to play and hug them. I wish it was that easy. I would have taken him in a heartbeat!*

Later, while we're in Binh's office going over some paperwork, a caregiver walks in with a bowl of some type of porridge and a big scoop spoon. She says this is Minh's lunch. I try to feed it to her but she won't take it. The social worker comes to assist. He says that because of her *harelip*, she lies flat on the floor to eat. *What!?!?* I try to lie her on the table but she starts screaming. *I feel very inept.* They take me to the nursery so the caregiver can show me how she's supposed to be fed. The woman squats on the floor with the food and tells Minh to lie down on the floor. They have a little pillow for her head. Minh still won't take it. They say she normally *takes her food* this way but with all the excitement...*This all makes me a little nervous. I have 4 other children, an experienced parent, but can't seem to be able to feed Minh.* We let her get up and go.

The cutest thing is *pee time.* They put those little toddlers on individual buckets lined up against the wall. Their little bottoms are suctioned right in the colorful bucket, their feet dangling, some not touching the floor. They just look at each other and babble. The staff leave them there until they *do their business.* None of them wear diapers. Minh won't sit on her bucket. *I think she's afraid she'll miss something!*

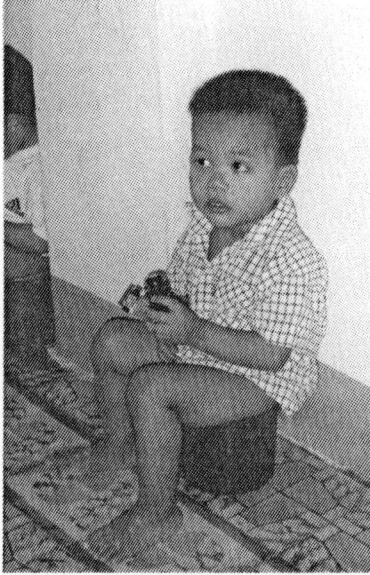

I see Phuong quietly suctioned in his little red bucket. We've been emailing his soon-to-be parents regularly. They're due to come to Vietnam next week to begin the finalization process. Phuong's new parents' names are Dayton and Tracy, so they plan to combine their names to call him Trayton. *Minh acts like his big sister. She pulls him around and away from stuff he isn't supposed to get into. Sweet! I can't wait to email them when we get back to the hotel.* They're anxiously waiting to hear from us. I get a good picture of Trayton in LeBinh's lap.

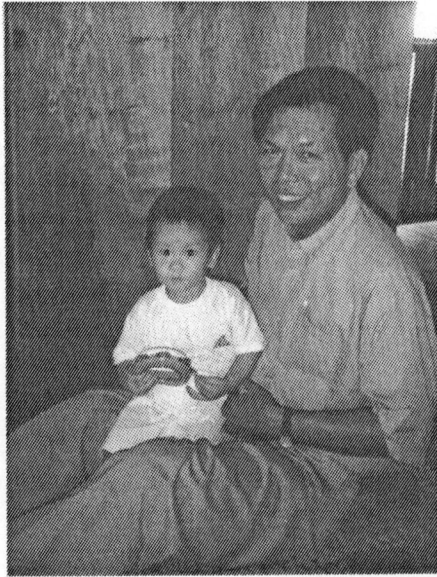

Le Binh comes in and tells us it's time to go to lunch. We get in the van with Minh. Our driver again follows Binh on his scooter. He has already ordered…We start with fish balls. *I couldn't chew them.* I tear them open and feed Minh the inside of a couple. *She likes food, not poured down her throat, but touching and holding it.* They then serve huge steamed shrimp. They're great! We have steamed rice, pieces of fish in brown sauce, vegetables and a soup with leafy green vegetables floating in it. Binh says a traditional Vietnamese meal is "soup, salty, and fried." There are no forks, just chopsticks. *I'm trying to keep Minh amused and I can't seem to pick up anything with my chopsticks.* Binh sees how much Minh loves trying food so he orders her some soup. It's a thick paste with fish morsels, along with some chewy pieces of eel. I feed her almost the whole bowl with a broad, deep spoon. Jimmy is expected to *party* with Binh and the guys that show up from Immigration. They order him beer after beer, CHEERS…After lunch, cigarettes come for the men. *Needless to say, Jimmy is a little tipsy after lunch.* They walk us to the van and Minh senses something happening. They tell us goodbye and give Minh one last hug and words of support. They tell us that she's very intelligent. Binh says she would have no future here. As Binh hands her back to me she screams and cries, not wanting to let him go. **He kisses her, hands her to me, says *"she has my heart"* and walks off.**

On the hour ride back to the Rex, I hold Minh in my lap, no car seat…She cries softly, looks out the window, looks in the back seat, everywhere for Binh, the director, anyone familiar. She's so sleepy, but she won't rest against my chest. She keeps nodding off, eventually falling to sleep, but restlessly jerking and groaning.

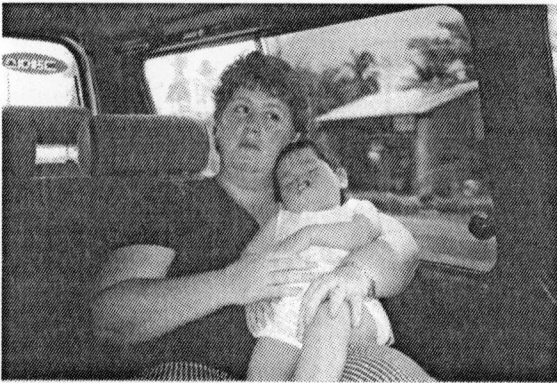

We get back to the hotel late afternoon. We bring soothing baby bath products from America. We just know she'll love soaking and playing in a bathtub, *something she isn't used to.* Well, she screams and is terrified! We make it fast and put a gown on her. She does like the frilly little pink nightgown. We try to hold her for a while but she doesn't like cuddling at this point. She loves her stroller. We decide to put some clothes on her and go to the shopping center across the street. *We cause quite a scene!* People act like they've never seen anyone with a disability or *defect* before. We buy a few souvenirs and go back up to our room early.

We order room service. Minh has a mango and scrambled eggs which she happily devours with her fingers. We order cheeseburgers *but I don't think it's beef so I pass.* Jimmy of course finishes them both. I fix Minh a bottle around 7:30PM. We cut a big hole in a nipple, but she won't drink it. She cries and grabs herself when she wets her diaper. She's used to it running down her leg if she has an accident. She's never worn a disposable diaper before. We show her it's okay and put a fresh one on her. *She keeps going to the door, pacing, and shifting her feet.* We try to play with her on the floor. She has fun, but is so sleepy. We put her in the crib we have sent up but she cries and cries. We end up putting her between us in the bed. She won't lie down, get comfortable…*She sits straight up, head bobbing until she finally gets so sleepy that we gently ease her down.* She kicks off covers, not used to them. She restlessly sleeps, sucking hard on her fingers. She puts 3-4 fingers in her nose/mouth area. *Jimmy and I just watch her sleep.* **What a day!**

Tuesday, May 22

We get up early and go up for breakfast. Every morning they set out an elaborate buffet with traditional Vietnamese dishes as well as omelettes, toast, etc. *Minh loves touching and trying all these different kinds of foods.* She eats a banana, mango, and some thinly-sliced meat. A Vietnamese man comes over and asks "Can she chew?" We explain that she has teeth and a few surgeries can correct the rest. *He smiles at us throughout breakfast. He's just curious I guess.*

We meet Mrs. Huong in the Rex lobby at 9AM. She looks over all of our paperwork, getting it in order for the *all-important* visa interview that will take place in a few days. We walk a couple of blocks to a photography studio. We take Minh upstairs for a picture to use for her visa. *It takes quite a few minutes to get her to face the correct way, not crying, and her hands not in her mouth.* We stroll around town for a few hours after leaving Mrs. Huong. *People stop and stare at her, cringe.* We come back in the lobby and check our email in the lounge. A group of *well-to-do* people stop and look right at her and rudely burst out laughing...Minh looks up at them from her stroller. *My heart aches for her! I can't tell if she's hurting. Hopefully, their stares and actions are things she can't understand.*

We go to our room and attempt to nap. We're trying to somewhat stay on her usual schedule. She cries and walks around holding a little cup. I put a little water in it but she spills it. We try different ways to get liquid down, without having her lie on the floor. *We finally figure it out, a straw!* We suction liquid in the straw then put it in her mouth to flow out. She loves this method. *I think she just loves drinking!* She's obviously very thirsty! *She looks like a hungry little bird, holding her head back with mouth open.* Jimmy feeds her half of a bottle this way. *We think she's finished.* Jimmy lies down on the floor. Minh goes over to him, pulls his head up. She has a crayon that she puts in her little cup and pretends to feed Jimmy, *grunting and making little chirping sounds.* **She wants more!** We get a bottle of water out and feed her, drop by drop through the straw.

She doesn't want to lie on the bed but she's so sleepy. She lets us hold her for a while. She sits right in the middle of the floor, bobbing her head until she literally falls asleep sitting up. We lay her right down where she is. We turn off the lights and even doze for an hour ourselves. *I turn on the light, expecting to see her sleeping soundly. She's sitting up in the middle of the floor. She has slowly shred a napkin into a million teeny pieces, quietly.* I pick her up and talk to her while some of the Rex staff prepare our daily afternoon tea. They bring hot tea and also coconuts. A man hacks off the top of the coconut, sticks a straw in, and hands it to us.

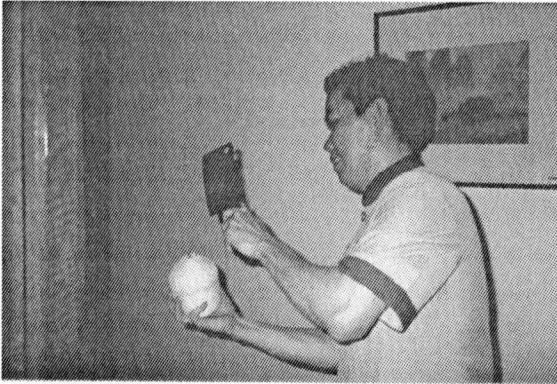

We get busy straw-feeding coconut juice to Minh. She loves it, can't get enough. He also brings a bunch of lychees which are delicious. Bananas are always kept in a basket in our room. They're very small compared to ours but they taste just like the regular-sized bananas.

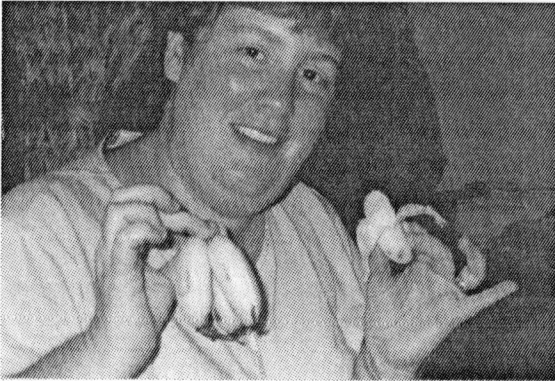

Minh loves playing with her crayons, not really coloring with them. She enjoys putting them in the box, taking them out, putting them all back in…*She makes sweet little coo sounds.* She smiles at us a lot more now. *When she's really tickled, she gives us the biggest grin!* You can see all the way down her nose, throat…when she puts that smile on.

We get dressed for dinner but go to a nearby shop first. Jimmy is trying to find him some sandals. He's much bigger than the typical Vietnamese man. They just look at his feet with wide eyes and shake their heads at his size 12s. He can wear tennis shoes to the pool or wherever else we go. We go up to dinner and Minh starts crying, and crying, and crying. That man that asked *if she could chew* comes right over, *thinking he's helpful,* and gives her a big, hard apple. We accept it but she can't possibly bite into that. We see the situation isn't working so we go back to our room. Minh shuffles back to our room, walks in and points to the stroller and grins real big. We put her in the stroller and head right back to the restaurant. *She sits in her stroller through the entire meal, through the entertainment, smiling and happily content, The music is beautiful and very unusual.* The instruments are strange, some crudely made and others with inlaid gems, *works of art.* The traditional dancers come out and Minh claps and sways to the music, *but of course never getting out of that stroller!*

I eat huge, grilled shrimp, *yes grilled*, not raw like in Bangkok. *Delicious!* Jimmy is eating huge prawns and lagostinos. *Our dinner is messy but wonderful!* I feed Minh some shrimp. *This night has been so great that we decide to top it off with a visit to the Paradise Lounge!?!?* This lounge is also where we use computers for emailing our children back in Pennsylvania staying with grandparents. There's a female singer, a cellist, and a couple of other instrumentalists. They're singing American tunes but with a *twangy* Vietnamese slant. It's funny to hear them sing a *"Sting"* or *"Beatles"* song with such drama and emotion.

We stroll outside and watch all of the activity. There are children selling postcards, fans, a book called **The Sorrow of War**. There are *very little ones* selling flowers. Any time we step a foot outside the hotel lobby, men follow Jimmy wanting to shine his shoes. *He has on canvas tennis shoes!?!?* We're walking on the sidewalk and a boy around 7 or 8 years old sees Minh and his eyes get huge! He walks right beside the stroller talking real loud, getting people's attention, to look at her. He's like a carnival barker announcing us as we pass. *Does Minh understand why? Do I?* Jimmy gets really angry but keeps control. The boy is walking so close to Minh that he's tripping over the stroller. We try to shoo him away. We finally find a store to duck into. We smile at Minh and kiss her sweet cheeks. **A little sparkle appears in those expressive eyes of hers.** *How is it possible to have so much love for this little girl? She's our daughter. I loved her before I even knew her, and I'll love her forever.*

Wednesday, May 23

Right after breakfast we meet our driver and guide in the lobby. We go to the History Museum first. It's amazing, and very informative. We then head to Chinatown, **Cholon**, a busy place! While in Cholon, we tour the **Thien Hau Pagoda** and the **Binh Tay Market**. We notice that the young women on scooters wear handkerchief masks and gloves pulled all the way up to their armpits. *It's definitely not cold!* The mask is for the pollution. Many men and all of the children wear them, too. The gloves are to keep the girls' skin as light as possible. *Our guide tells us that the lighter the skin, the prettier the girl.* They very much prefer light skin. They think we're foolish to lie out in the sun baking, trying to tan. They're just the opposite.

We tour the imposing Notre Dame Cathedral before going to the Municipal Post Office. *We wonder why anyone would want to make the post office a stop on a Saigon tour but it turns out to be very interesting.* We come up to **Buu Dien**, the post office. It's a grand old colonial building with the contemporary architectural style of Europe. Its eclectic style was surprisingly created in 1891, with an iron and glass ceiling designed by Gustave Eiffel. There are huge maps of Vietnam on both sides of the main entrance and a huge portrait of *Uncle Ho* in the rear. We see people laboriously painting glue to the back of stamps and envelopes. Glued stamps are only just beginning to make an appearance in Vietnam. *Now I understand why my intricately detailed stationary I bought yesterday came with what I thought were cheap envelopes. The envelopes are all thin with no glue on the back!?!?* They're doing more than postal business. People are studying, using phones, buying books and planning trips with the help of agents.

The last stop on this whirlwind tour is a workshop that crafts beautiful lacquerware. We're shown several different techniques, some using inlaid mother-of-pearl and others using delicate egg shells to create inlaid flowers and traditional scenes. We're the only people touring out back where workers are busy with their art and the only ones buying in the shop. The workers ask many questions about Minh. They aren't gawking or showing faces of disdain, but are truly interested. They ask *"Can it be fixed in America?"…"Can she talk, chew, drink milk that is healthy"…*They keep rubbing her head saying *"lucky baby."* One young woman bends down and coos with her for quite a while and touches her face, saying she's intelligent. She asks if she has good health otherwise. She also asks if we can afford to educate her. *She rubs Minh's cheek speaking softly to her in Vietnamese. Minh smiles at her.* We buy several things before getting back in the car. We buy beautiful inlaid combs and barrettes. We also decide to splurge and get a small folding screen. The wood has been glossed numerous times. The mother-of-pearl inlay depicts country village scenes. Our last purchase is a small ashtray for Jimmy, for when he indulges in his rare past time of smoking cigars.

Our guide explains many things and we ask him a zillion questions. We ask about marriage. He says that when a man gets to be about 30 years old it's probably time to get married. They choose their own mates in the city. In the country or villages, they marry younger and they're pre-arranged. Looks are a big deal! He matter-of-factly says that the country girls aren't as pretty. A man might go to the country to see a girl that's open for marriage. *"He looks at her face and if she's ugly he doesn't want to marry her of course...turns around and leaves."*

Contrary to the books I read, he tells us that there is **no free education**. Even the public or state schools cost. The private schools are very expensive but excellent. If a family can't afford a state school, the children just don't go. He goes on to explain that everyone in the city works for the government. Vietnamese can have 2 children max. If they have more than 2 children, deductions will be made from their salary. The farmers in the country and the workers in the remote villages typically determine for themselves the number of children they'll have. It isn't regulated out there.

We learn a lot from our guide. He likes practicing his English. He tells us that a Vietnamese man can support a wife, 1-2 children, and own a scooter for about 11/2 million dong a month. *That's about US$100!* Entire families ride on their one scooter. The most we see on one is five. We also see a man driving his scooter and the *mama* on back holding their teeny baby. Their typical work week is Monday—Friday from 7:30-5PM with 11/2 hours midday to go home for lunch and a quick nap. After work, men like to sit in the coffee shops, talk to friends, and drink beer. *The owner hires pretty girls only or the men won't come back. The girls will sit and talk with the patron.*

Our Saigon tour is officially over so we're taken back to the Rex. On the way back, Minh throws up mangoes and a lot of water. We don't want to mess up the car so the closest thing we grab for her to throw up in is the sack from the lacquerware shop, full of our carefully wrapped purchases. *Oh well.* We go up to the room, clean her off and start unwrapping and cleaning our lacquer gifts. Minh isn't used to riding in an enclosed car. Many Vietnamese get carsick. There aren't many cars. *They're accustomed to riding on scooters, no helmets, just constant fresh air.* We then send out laundry. They leave a wicker basket in the room.

They bring your clothes back the next morning all clean and starchy pressed in the same little basket.

Because of the heat and for fear of dehydration, we drink bottled water constantly. We've been warned against drinking faucet or tap water. We're even supposed to use the bottled water to brush our teeth but we don't and we haven't gotten sick yet. *Knock on wood!* On the way to our room we look down into a separate courtyard and see a hotel gardener watering and *tediously trimming* the Bonsai trees.

Our fax machine comes to life around 3PM to give us the message that Mrs. Huong wishes to see us in the lobby. She tells us that there's a mistake on some of the paperwork. It lists Minh as a male, instead of a female. She assures us that she can call *people* she knows to get it easily corrected. She arranges a guide and driver for us tomorrow. We go to the big market across the street for more souvenir shopping. *Minh loves the little outfits we brought for her. She eagerly changes into her little dresses, matching socks, hair bows, and hats…She points to the flowers on her dresses and makes a sweet, chirping sound. She's "all girl," twirling around and around in her dress like a ballerina.* In a little grocery, we find baby cereal mix. It has big rice bits, spinach, grated carrots, shredded chicken…just add warm water. We also buy a little plastic bowl and spoon. We go back to our room and she laps up 2 packages of it. We order room service for a quiet dinner in the room. We eat 2 filet mignons and fries…for $10, total. Jimmy straw-feeds her a half-bottle of formula. Minh has fun playing with her crayons and a little toy scooter. I go down to the **Paradise Lounge** to check our email on an available computer. There's a message from my children and my mom! *It feels so good hearing from them.* They're having a lot of fun! We try to write to them every day relaying our adventures.

Minh has a rough night at first. She usually gets tense, but this is even more than usual. She cries and cries. She just looks at Jimmy, then me…She looks so precious, all clean in her tiny pink nightgown and little white socks. *I just wish she knew how much we love her so she would feel more comfortable with us.* She won't let me even attempt to console her. Jimmy puts her on his chest but she doesn't lay her head down. She's so sleepy, head bobbing…She wakes up after sleeping for about an hour and starts kicking and shrieking, looking at us and crawling backward away from us. We finally just put her on the floor. She stares at the little night light, bobbing her sleepy head. After about $1/2$ hour she starts softly whimpering. Jimmy picks her up. She shrieks at first but she calms and the whole process starts again…her not totally relaxing…dozing, jerking awake, looking at us…She finally falls asleep again and stays in a deep sleep.

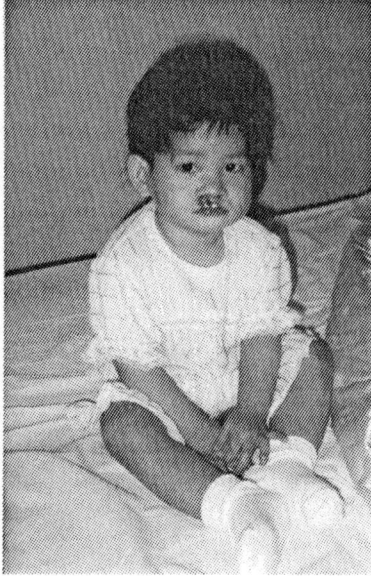

I feel so sorry for her. She has such fun during the day, out and about, laughing, eating, getting to know us. Night, though, is a different story! Minh is experiencing a flood of feelings which are much more confusing and frightening because she hasn't yet learned to rely on us, her new parents. *Even though my heart breaks to see her this way, it truly is a good sign.* Her *"homesickness"* at night shows me how much she was loved by the people at the orphanage, and how much she loved them. Her actions reveal that she attached and shared a deep, trusting bond with her *"family"* at the orphanage. At least we know that she's capable of bonding, making strong attachments. *She'll grieve for the people she's physically leaving, but in time she'll bond with us.* Jimmy and I love her very much.

It's 4AM and I'm sitting in the bathroom trying to be quiet. Jimmy is also awake but lying down trying to sleep a little more. It's so hard to get used to the time change.

Thursday, May 24

Minh is sleeping deeply this morning. We actually have to wake her. We go up to the fancy 5th floor for breakfast as usual. There are ants all over the tablecloths. I noticed some yesterday but not quite as many as today. *They act as if it's normal. I guess it would have to be in a tropical climate such as this!* Our waiter walks around the table and flicks them off or picks up a place mat and shakes them off. *Whew! That's a little hard to get used to.*

We meet our guide and the private car that has previously been arranged, a full day for just $65. He drives about 11/2 hours to the underground village at Ben Duoc in the **Cu Chi** District. This is amazing! *For $1 a bullet, they would allow us to fire an AK-47 assault rifle. We pass!* While there, Minh gets bitten by a bug and her whole forehead and chin get red and swollen. After exploring this elaborate network of tunnels, we ride for another 11/2 hours to **Tay Ninh**. We're going to the **Cao Dai Holy See**, which resembles *a bizarre-like Disneyland with a religious twist* about 2 $^1/_2$ hours outside Ho Chi Minh City and within sight of the Cambodian border.

On the way to Tay Ninh, the countryside is packed with lush ricefields, where water buffalo lounge and women are bent double harvesting rice. As we near, we see **Nui Ba Den** *(Black Lady Mountain). There are several*

versions of how the mountain got its name, but they all center on a princi-
pled lady who chose death to dishonor. The Khmers regard the mountain as
holy, complete with a shrine near the top. It towers 2,953 feet, piercing the
skyline between Cambodia and Vietnam. Tay Ninh's province borders
Cambodia and many of the people there are Khmer, with a small Cham
minority. In 1978, border skirmishes in this region were cited as the reason
for Vietnam's occupation of Cambodia.

We're then taken to lunch. The guide and driver let us out and
leave. They'll come back in an hour or so. **To get to this *nice* restau-**
rant, Jimmy steps in a sloshy mud puddle right in front of the
entrance. As we enter, a skinny half-bald chicken runs right out of
the front door! *We just watch it, look at each other and laugh, then walk*
on in.

Because we're American, they know we like air condition. The lady
that greets us leads us straight to a private air conditioned room.
Jimmy and I eat fried rice. Minh eats scrambled eggs. For dessert, they
bring a tray of fresh fruit. The smelly but delectable durian is delicious.
We eat a bunch of lychees. We feed Minh dragon fruit. *She just slurps*
and smacks. It's by far her favorite! The dragon fruit is hot pink, almost
the size of a large avocado and very vulgar-looking with horns and
uneven pieces on the outside. The inside is clear white with small dark
seeds. The family that runs the restaurant is very friendly. Our guide

comes back to pick us up and the women ask her many questions about Minh. An older woman hugs me tight, saying "thank you, thank you..." *Minh plays it up, going to each lady to be held.*

On the way back to Saigon, it's so enchanting to see the green, fertile rice paddies and the very small children serenely leading water buffaloes. We ask about all of these clear white circles drying on numerous bamboo screens in the sun. She tells us they're freshly made rice cakes. They use the thin cake, put rice and vegetables in, roll it up and dip in fish sauce. There are villages that specialize in the making and sale of the rice cakes. In this one village, there are 1,000s of transparent cakes drying. I tell our guide that I want to see where and how they're made. She tells us that the villagers just make them in their own homes. I persistently ask if I can go in a house...Our driver pulls over to a home, doesn't know them, asks if we could see this rice process and her house. She tells him that it's nap time, but one of us can come in for a few minutes.

I walk across a crude log bridge to get to the house. It's midday so there are three people not sleeping, but lying on the one big bed watching a small television. She shows me her kitchen which is a couple of holes in the floor with wood fires, a few concrete blocks, and rice plastered everywhere and on everything. I thank her and get back in the car. We drive a few feet and come up to a roadside stand selling rice cakes, so we get out and buy a few packages. We buy the sweet ones that they've embellished with cashews. They're hard, crunchy, and very good. We get to the city and simply riding in this traffic is an adventure in itself.

We go to the roof-top restaurant tonight, in the Rex, for dinner. Minh is *feeling her cheerios.* She's coming out of her shell, personality shining through. She smiles real big at everybody. She sits there and flings her toys real fast all over the floor, *just like a typical 2 year-old.* Her mouth is very swollen and scabby. *No matter what she looks like though, you can't not smile at her when she gives you one of those huge grins!* She gets especially excited when a chef comes to our table and makes us a special pineapple flambe. She shrieks, points, and claps. She cuts her eyes at me and giggles. I wiggle my finger at her and get closer, closer, until I tickle her with it. She laughs and laughs! I wiggle my finger and she watches it out of the corner of her eye and starts giggling before I even tickle her. She wiggles her finger at me now. She has some crazy, funny looks. She's such a sassy little thing. *We call her Miss Sassafrass!*

Minh's mouth is really looking bad lately, even bleeding. She goes to bed good but wakes up several times crying. I get a tissue and wipe off the goo and blood. I notice a big white spot under the right side of her nose. I turn on the light and show Jimmy. *I would have been crying, too! It's a big tooth that has broken through.* Now she has a tooth that looks like it's coming out of her nostril. We'll need to get her to a doctor fast when we get back to Pennsylvania.

Friday, May 25

She wakes up early this morning. She drinks a whole cup of formula. *We have it figured out now.* Instead of a straw, we use a bigger medicine measurer, long plastic with spoon part having a lip on both sides. *Perfect!* We go up to eat. *Minh is pretty lively!* A group of Vietnamese women sit at the table next to us but get up and move. A couple *almost* sit down but choose another table across the room. The women stare at us from afar.

We meet Mrs. Huong in the lobby around 10AM. She tells us how happy Le Binh is that Minh has found a family. *He loves her so much!* Nobody wants her for 2 years but then her photo appears in the Holt magazine (**Hi Families**) as a *"waiting child."* Mrs. Houng says that when Binh received his magazine he got so upset because he didn't think it was a cute photo. He kept saying that he sent several that were more favorable. He was so worried that no one would want her. The social worker, director, etc. all share a special affection for her. They say that because she was *unlucky* they spent extra time with her, teaching her things. *Their efforts are obvious! She's most certainly a child that has been loved.* She's very intelligent, too, and has the personality and fortitude that will carry her far.

We get a taxi and follow Mrs. Huong on her scooter. She takes us to a market.

When we get there, she leaves on her scooter to go back to work. We buy some ornate chopsticks with ivory ends and detailed artwork on the sticks themselves. One shopkeeper is very nice. She gives Minh a toy loved by many Vietnamese children. It's a wood-carved toad with a scaly back. It comes with a stick that you rake down its back making the deep, *ribbet-sound* that toads make when they know rain is coming. The toad is the symbol of rain in this country. This toy keeps Minh occupied for a large chunk of time.

A woman probably in her 50s sees Minh and follows us. She has a long walking stick that she uses to point at Minh while laughing real loud. I really don't understand…and again we try not get angry. We're through shopping anyway.

We're not sure where the Rex is and there isn't a taxi within sight so we just head in the direction we think is right. *I'm so HOT!* We make it back to the Rex around noon. We feed her some formula and she lies down and goes to sleep. *So do we!* I kind of like these midday naps. We go to sleep watching sumo wrestling. There are about 4 channels. One of them is Asian MTV. *I have to say I'm sick to death of Janet Jackson. They play her videos almost every other song it seems like.*

We wake up and walk outside for a stroll. It looks like everyone is out! It's Friday night and there is activity and excitement everywhere. We take pictures of the People's Committee building with the blood red Communist flag flying high above it. We also take some shots of the Municipal Opera House. There are people following us, *as usual,* little children selling postcards, balloons, flowers, noodles…*It feels cozy warm outside, not hot.* The daily afternoon rains help cool things down. Everyone likes coconut juice. People are selling it everywhere on the streets. They hack off the top with a huge knife, stick a straw in and *viola!* They drink that for a cool refreshment like we drink iced tea or soft drinks. We also try a popular sugarcane drink. *I like it because it's sickenly sweet, but Jimmy prefers the coconut juice.*

We watch the people eating dinner, squatting on the sidewalks, laughing and talking with each other. We turn a corner and see a Baskin Robbins' sign. *Is it a mirage? HA!* We run in and eat bowls of Rocky Road and Rainbow Sherbert. *Minh just can't lick it fast enough. She really enjoys her sweet, cool sherbert.* We walk around some more. *I take photos of children. They love to pose!*

One little girl, maybe 4 years old, keeps looking at Minh, in a sweet way, not critical or teasing. She pulls her mom over and gives her balloon to Minh. *It's so sweet!* It's a big, red heart balloon on a stick with little yellow balloons on the outside. *Minh's eyes light up!* She keeps a tight grip on her new balloon, smiling and enjoying our night out. We go to the government shop and buy her two little 18k bangle bracelets. Our other children had baby rings. A lot of Vietnamese children wear gold bangles and earrings.

We come in later than usual and order room service. Jimmy orders fried rice and baked macaroni and cheese for us. *It's really good!* Later, I go down to the lounge and email our children. My mom and the children have sent us messages. *We miss them but are enjoying getting to know our little girl and her country.* I go back up and Minh is eating Pringles. Ever since she tasted one, she eats them pretty much nonstop.

We try and get her ready for bed. *I so much want her to enjoy a good, warm bath but she screams throughout the process.* I even get in there with her and Jimmy stays right there but that plan doesn't work either.

She'll eventually get used to baths, in due time I guess. She runs right over to her frilly pajamas, though. *She loves them!* She has a little cold. She isn't used to the air condition yet. She goes to sleep fast but on the floor. We corral her in with pillows and let her stay there peacefully. Jimmy goes down to the lobby and arranges for a driver to take us to the beach tomorrow.

Saturday, May 26

After eating breakfast, we meet our driver in the lobby around 9AM, no English guide today. After 2 hours of unbelievable scenery, we come to VungTau. The beaches are beautiful! The driver drops us off at sandy Bien Bong on the South China Sea and parks to wait for us. *The sand is warm and white. The water is clean and clear with small, ripply waves.* At first Minh is scared of the water, especially the waves. She likes us carrying her out into the water, though. She sits at the edge and plays with little beach toys and pats her hands in the water. A cute Asian woman and her family are next to us on the beach. She smiles at Minh and she hops up and toddles right over there. We talk with that family for a while. Midday, a woman strolls down the beach with lunch. She sets her food out and people go right over for **pho**, *squatting on the sand at this Vietnamese concession stand.*

We're the only white people to be seen. *Everyone stares at us, they're so curious.* Vietnamese are very small people. They keep asking if they can have their picture made with Jimmy. A group of men want their picture made again and again with him. They stand there hugging Jimmy, grinning real big and giving a thumbs-up sign. *Funny!*

They have no concept of *personal space*. Several women come right up and touch my hair *(it's red)* without asking. It doesn't scare me *just startles a bit.* One woman keeps touching my face. They like white skin. *That's me!?!?* My fair skin and bright hair evidently fascinate them.

On a mountain to the right is a huge white sculpture of Jesus with outstretched arms. After a few hours at the beach, we change and find our driver. He takes us to a little restaurant. Minh has vegetable soup and we have fried rice. The restaurant faces the water. We watch the boats making their way to the ocean. *The boats sailing to the ocean are adorned with huge blue and red eyes painted right on the front, helping to guide their way.* We are then taken to the Whale Temple and onto the White Villa.

*Farther down the coast is the White Villa, **Bach Ding**. It's set in a mature garden with stunning views of the South China Sea. This is French colonial architecture at its best, appointed with intricate art nouveau ornamentation. It was built in 1898-1916 as a summer residence for the then governor-general of Indochina (Paul Doumer). Emperor Thanh Thai was kept here under house arrest in 1907, and in the late 1960s-70s, President Thieu, the South Vietnamese head of state, used it as a vacation home, as did government officials post-1975. It's now an eclectic museum with exhibits ranging from a Dong Son drum, Oc Eo artifacts, Khmer bronzes, to the major attraction—exquisite Qing Dynasty Chinese porcelain rescued from a shipwreck. In all, 28,000 pieces of Holland-bound export sank off the Southern coast of Vietnam. Originating from South China, the pieces were produced for the European market, some depicting Dutch canal houses.*

On the way back from Vung Tau, there's a big storm, lots of thunder, lightening and pounding rain. *I think all these scooter riders will have to find shelter.* Everyone pulls over to the side of the road, dons parkas, and keeps right on traveling on their scooters. *We see one man slide and wreck his scooter on the wet street but it doesn't look like he's hurt.* We're all a little sunburned from our time at the beach, but it's a feel-good healthy burn. We go to bed early tonight. *Minh sleeps soundly, but still on the hard floor!?!?*

Sunday, May 27

We get up and eat breakfast as usual. She enjoys her breakfast of fish porridge and fruit. *We go shopping and have a lazy afternoon.* Even though it's raining, we walk around a little outside. While Minh is napping midday, Jimmy goes to the market. She wakes up and we walk to the Continental Hotel.

Built in 1890, the Continental is the pre-eminent historic hotel in Saigon, of Somerset Maugham's Quiet American *fame. Its lovely colonial facade leads into an overly ornate lobby. The rooms are huge with high ceilings and decorated with red velveteen curtains and red carpets.*

The Williams, Trayton's mom and dad, check in around 4PM. We can't wait to meet them. They're exhausted from their trip so Tracy is asleep. We talk to Dayton for a while. We shop for more souvenirs and watch a wedding preparation in the Rex's open courtyard. *The bride and groom are wearing typical formal Western attire. They're very excited that I want to snap their photo.* We order and eat in the room again, filet mignon and more baked macaroni and cheese. *I had planned on losing weight while here. HA!HA!HA!*

Mrs. Huong calls and makes plans to meet us for paperwork tomorrow morning. Tracy Williams calls and is anxious to hear about Phuong, *now called Trayton.* Their process begins early tomorrow morning with the trip to the orphanage. We'll meet tomorrow afternoon.

We have to clean, more or less, debride Minh's mouth/nose area each evening. She cries and just looks at us. She probably wonders why we'd want to hurt her. We have to do it, though, because it looks like it could get infected so easy! The air condition, dry air, and a big tooth erupting have made it rather messy. So, we clean and put antibiotic ointment on it. *I can't wait until we get her to a doctor in America. We really need some guidance on how to best care for her.* We give her a little Tylenol tonight to help.

Jimmy and I reflect on our day. *When we overlook the negative reactions to Minh, it's really nice here.* We talked with a cyclo driver today that could speak English pretty good. *It was fascinating hearing about his life!* We see the women carrying fresh food and coconut milk balanced on their thin shoulders in baskets. The little girls were out selling their postcards and fans. They followed us talking and asking questions about America. Some of the child beggars have *heart wrenching stories* but we abstain from giving any of them money. If we gave one child money, there would be a swarm surrounding us in seconds.

We sure do miss our children at home. We've been emailing daily, though. We really can't wait to get Minh home. She'll love her brothers and sister, and the puppies. She points to puppies in her books and makes little barking sounds. **The country is beautiful and we're having an awesome adventure! We're just ready to reunite our family and start this new phase of life—all of us!**

We watch whatever is on television—a BBC show about *"the new face of leprosy"*—before drifting off to sleep.

Monday, May 28

She sure is snoozing! She didn't wake at all during the night. *This is the longest, most serene rest she's had.* She sleeps until 8AM. *The staff at the 5th floor restaurant will think we checked out, considering we're usually there by 6:15AM!?!?* We walk around the hotel and meet Mrs. Huong at the designated time (1PM) to go to the police station.

It's raining, really storming. We go to the police station to submit dossier paperwork for Minh's visa. Mrs. Huong puts our papers on the counter and we sit down to wait for our name to be called. There are a lot of people waiting! *Two policemen get into a fuss. More people get involved…They put their paperwork down and all go out the back door. We look at each other wondering what in the world is going on.* Mrs. Huong finds out that the fuss is over *who really won the checker game* that was played during lunch time. They went to finish the game. We wait like everyone else. They come back 10 minutes later and start work!?!? When they call Minh's name, Jimmy goes up and shows our passports. *That's it for now.*

We see a cute girl every day, 10 years old. Her name is *Ha*! She has trimmed bangs, dresses very conservatively and clean, always selling books and postcards. A woman from the hotel tells us that she gets beaten if she doesn't sell enough. *She's a character!* You can't help but love her! She says she's selling things to afford school. She has great English which she learns from talking with tourists.

We meet the Williams at our hotel. They have Trayton now. It's still raining so we don't walk around very much. We all come back to our room for a couple of hours. Trayton and Minh play and play with their new toys. Mostly Minh feeds Trayton little mini Ritz crackers and Pringles, *and he smiles*. She resumes her *Big Sis* role she obviously had at the orphanage. Trayton is 6 months younger.

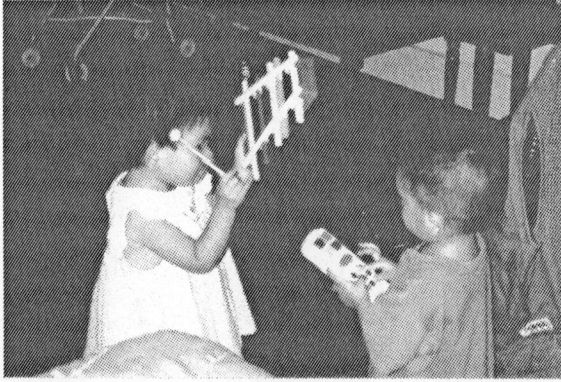

At 5:30PM, we go to Rex's roof-top restaurant. It's early so we're the only ones there. *That's probably a good thing! HA!* We order spring rolls as appetizers. They're delicious, stuck in a candle-lit pineapple with toothpicks. *Trayton and Minh love them!* They smile and *hoot* at each other. Trayton is throwing Tracy's spaghetti. HA! *They're a riot!* After dinner, we walk them back to their hotel for the night. The Williams live in Sioux Falls, South Dakota. He's a veterinarian, and with Tracy's help, they own and run an *all-pet* animal hospital, He's also the resident vet for the Sioux Falls Zoo.

There are youth here in Saigon staying at the Rex competing for the Taekwondo World Cup. They practice sometimes in the courtyard. I've seen teams from Canada, Korea, Brazil, Iran, Italy, Japan, Turkey…

Tuesday, May 29

We eat breakfast around 7AM. Minh eats a lot of pork porridge. We then go down to the lobby to arrange for a guide and driver. He gets us everything we need by 9AM. The guide is great, very knowledgeable and his English is thankfully understandable. He's a local University student.

We head for the Mekong Delta. It takes about 2 hours to get to **My Tho**. *My Tho reveals the beauty of the Mekong Delta.* We get on a boat that circles around the fabulous patchwork of fruit orchards on Dragon, Turtle, Lion, and Phoenix Islands that lie midstream between My Tho and the province of **Ben Tre**.

The water is choppy. It looks like it may storm. We get in a small, motorized boat. There's a man driving the boat and a woman fixing us fresh coconut juice. We get off the boat and step onto an island, Phuong Island. **Phuong Island** is home to an offbeat religious sect set up three decades ago by the eccentric Coconut Monk, **Ong Dao Dua**. *We walk through amazing ripe orchards of papayas, dragon fruit, mangoes, lychees, pineapple…longans, sapodillas, guava, rambutans…We see island people working, playing, living. We go in one home and a man is squatting busily preparing rice, probably for rice wine. We sit down at a little makeshift café and sample all the delicious varieties of fruit. Minh just eats and eats! She's humming, thoroughly enjoying herself. Everyone is very nice.*

There are 2 other tourists. One of them, a Chinese man, comes over and asks if we're American. He tells us that he works for a newspaper and asks if he can take a picture of Jimmy and Minh…he says because "he is so nice to the unlucky baby." Of course Minh gives him one of her famous, enormous grins as soon as she sees his camera. We then walk around the island. There are a few monkeys but they're chained to the trees.

I want to see the island in more depth. I love seeing people in their daily habitats. Our English guide arranges a sampan for us. A man helps us in his little boat and we go through canals, deeper into the island. It's fascinating! We wear straw coolie hats so snakes won't fall on our heads as we're paddled through the thin canals and thick foliage. We get out and talk to the people. There are people tending bee hives. Every home has a few hives for their own enjoyment. We taste some bread with fresh honey.

We're shown 2 kinds of coconuts, land and water coconuts. At one home, they're making candy out of the coconut. It's real sticky, like taffy. Some batches are strictly coconut. Other batches have chocolate and

bananas added. They take it by boat to the nearest city to sell. We buy some warm, freshly made candy. Minh sucks on this for the rest of the afternoon.

    They use the coconuts for all kids of things. We see a man carving the shells into cooking utensils. We meet little kids on the beaten down dirt paths and they love when I take their pictures. We stop at one man's home and he's busy making the rice/snake wine that's so commonplace in this country. He pulls out a huge home-brewed batch that's obviously been fermenting for quite some time, maybe too long. This wine is in a gigantic glass jar. We see dead snakes coiled around in the bottom. Jimmy knows that he'll have to take a drink in order not to offend, because everyone has been so nice and hospitable. **When the man opens the jar to dip some out for Jimmy, we see a dead chicken floating in the top. Jimmy closes his eyes and downs it from the dirty, little teacup he is handed.** *We did get immunized against Hepatitis A and B, didn't we!?!? Whew! We figure that we've seen enough. We get into our little sampan which takes us to the motorized boat. We then go back to My Tho. We find our driver snoozing in a hammock, waiting.*

They take us to lunch. Our guide orders our meals and leaves us there. First, a girl comes over with an elephant ear fish. It's huge! She doesn't talk. She takes rice paper, puts in cucumber, carrots and slivers of fish. She rolls them up and shows us how to dip in the fish sauce. It's really good. She keeps rolling and putting them on our plates. On Minh's plate, the girl puts thin pieces of fish. Every now and then, Minh hands us little bones that are in her mouth!?!? Next, she brings bits of chicken that we dip in another sauce. She then brings out a hot ball that she cuts in half and folds over. There's sauce in this ball. After folding, she cuts it into strips. It's so warm and sweet, sticky sweet rice. She brings out huge steamed shrimp next. Are the courses ever going to end? She stands there, peels them, and puts them on our plates. I don't think I want the courses to stop.

She brings out a big bowl of boiling hot soup. She puts some in a bowl for each of us, over rice. It contains different kinds of vegetables and some little pork balls that are tied with strips of seaweed made to look like tiny presents. She brings another dish from the kitchen and stirs in little morsels of meat, in a barbecue-type sauce. We ask her what it is and she makes a barking noise. **I almost gag!** *I take it that I'm now eating some yellow-haired dog with my chopsticks!?!? We're so full! Lastly, she brings out a plate of those yummy mini bananas. We generously tip the restaurant workers and go in search of our guide and driver. Late afternoon, we head back to Ho Chi Minh City.*

We immediately call the Williams and meet them outside our hotel. Trayton is in his stroller. We stroll all around taking in the sights. We show them the Baskin Robbins and of course have some, *yes, even after all of that food!* Minh and Trayton smile at each other, lick their ice cream, and make chirping noises.

We go up to our room pretty late. We try again to give her a warm bath. She doesn't scream this time. *She won't sit down but she's not screaming…it's a start.* Her skin is so soft. We put her favorite nightgown on and let her play for a while. She's so funny, has so much personality. She dances, points, chirps, *so curious about every minute thing.* Her facial expressions are hilarious! *Her siblings are going to love her!* She giggles and runs around. She eventually tires and falls asleep. She'll only sleep on the hard, *yet carpeted,* floor. At least she's comfortably sleeping, even if it's not in a bed.

Wednesday, May 30

We get up early and eat breakfast upstairs. Two boys from the Japanese taekwondo team sit with us. They're quiet at first but begin telling us all about their matches and grueling practices.

We meet the Williams at 9AM and get a taxi to the zoo. It's fun. The children enjoy it and it's a nice day to be outside. We get back in time to meet Mrs. Huong in the lobby. We go to Immigration, hopefully to get Minh's passport. *We get through all the formalities without a hitch.* We go directly to the hospital for the medical exam, required to get a visa. ***They just look at her and ask if we're sure we want her.*** They tell us that she has a harelip—*in case we haven't noticed.* She's nice but does a very quick exam. We request medicine for the infected insect bites on her chin and forehead. *I think she has impetigo. She doesn't understand what I'm asking for. We need an antibiotic.* She says Minh has a cold and maybe a fever from the air condition!?!? She gives us a prescription and we leave, with a paper that says Minh is clear *medically* to leave the country. We stop at a couple of *pharmacies* before we find one that can fill the prescription. *The pharmacies are road-side stores or stands that have precious little inventory.* We get back to the hotel around 5PM. Dayton tells us later that the medicine isn't an antibiotic but a diluted hydrogen peroxide.

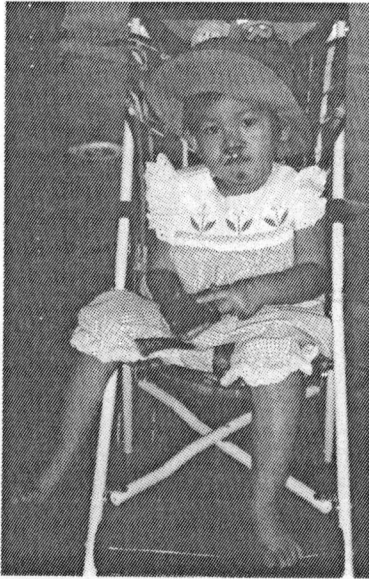

We call the Williams and meet them at a restaurant, a fancy one with cloth tablecloths, napkins, and chandeliers. Minh and Trayton have a wild time! We all order and are eating and talking, *having a great time*. I'm talking with Dayton and something falls from the ceiling and plops right on the top of his head. He looks up and I jump away from him. *It's a humongous cockroach! Without missing a beat in conversation, he knocks it off and kicks it away from the table. We get so tickled!* He says that it isn't the first time that has happened to him, *working at the zoo and all*. A few minutes later, the children see lime green geckos crawling on the walls around the light. *They're pointing and babbling. We finish up fast and get out of there!* They come up to our room for a while and Minh and Trayton play. *It's raining so hard!*

Later, Minh goes to bed. *It takes a while but she eventually conks out.* Jimmy and I talk about our day. We make good and fast friends with the Williams. We've only known them for a short time but feel very close and comfortable with them. ***You get to know someone real fast when traveling together in a distant country...***

Thursday, May 31

We get up early and eat by ourselves. We meet Mrs. Huong in the lobby at 7:30AM. This is the big day, when we apply for Minh's long-awaited visa, *the last step in getting her out of Vietnam.*

With all of our visa interview paperwork in hand, we get in a taxi to go to the U.S. Consulate. We wait in a short line for a while. Vietnamese guards come out and let Jimmy and Minh in. *I tell them that I'm with them but they shoo me back in line.* They search Jimmy, Minh, the stroller…*They even dig out Minh's Pringles.* They then let me in. They thoroughly search me and take my camera. We rejoin and wait in a room for them to call us. The United States no longer has an embassy in this country.

The former U.S. Embassy, now known as the U.S. Consulate, was completed in 1967, one of several diplomatic buildings designed by Edward Durrell Stone. The very next year millions of television viewers watched agape as a Viet Cong special force broke into the embassy grounds during the Tet Offensive. This building was also in the spotlight in 1975. The North Vietnamese army were rolling into Saigon. Thousands of panicking Vietnamese were trying to join the desperately retreating U.S. personnel, who were being shuttled by helicopter to aircraft carriers at sea. At dawn on April 30, the U.S. Ambassador swept into the helicopter. No one can forget the image just seconds later of that last helicopter leaving the grounds carrying a man aloft on a rope.

After our names are called, we're led to a small room with a window. The interview goes smoothly. Most of the questions are geared toward Minh's abandonment. *They're trying to ensure that she is indeed an orphan, eligible for adoption.* The American woman conducting the interview is very thorough but exceedingly nice and considerate. We have to talk through the bullet-proof glass. *Minh hoots like an owl the whole time because the echos in the room fascinate her.* The woman explains the process of getting her out of Vietnam and into the United States. She'll be considered an immigrant until we reach Minneapolis, the first touch-down in America. **Because of the new citizenship law,**

she'll be right then and there an American citizen! We're required to finalize the adoption again in the U.S. so we can legally change her name and request a PA birth certificate. It's a pretty day and we're done early. We decide to walk back to the Rex.

We call the Williams and all do a little shopping. We see Ha and she walks with us. We buy Minh several silk **ao dais**, with beaded slippers for each outfit! Trayton is outfitted with a spiffy silk get-up. We try a new restaurant on the corner. We have pizza with pineapples and pork. Delicious! Minh and Trayton eat spring rolls. They're tightly wrapped with the large shrimp tail hanging out. *Minh eats them and spits the tails out on her plate.* It's a modern cafe. We end our lunch with huge banana splits.

We go our separate ways for nap time. Minh screams bloody murder when we try to lay her down. *She would rather sit straight up in the floor, letting her eyes droop and head bob.* Jimmy tries to ease her down when she's practically asleep but she jerks awake and starts screaming. He reads her a picture book that she *usually* enjoys but she refuses to relax, knowing she'll nod off. I pick her up and hold her. She kicks and screams but quietens down after about 10 minutes. I put her on our bed. While she naps, Jimmy goes to the fitness center to work out.

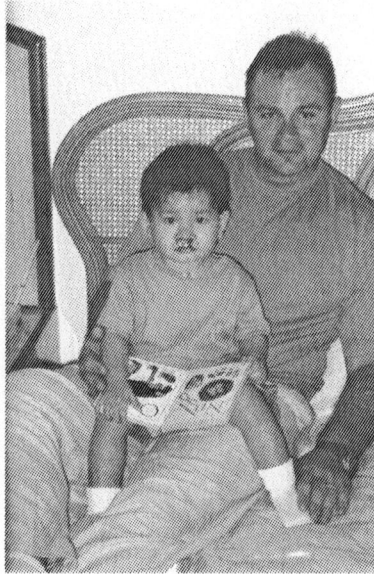

She sleeps for 3 hours! She eats some of the chunky rice cereal before we go over to the Continental. The Williams' suite is very nice. They have a sitting room. The rain is pouring down! We play in their room for a while. We walk to a local bookstore. Around 6PM we decide to try the supposedly American fried chicken from *Chicken Town*. We take it back to the Continental. The chicken and fries are pretty good. *The children love the fries! They have fun playing and fighting.* Trayton has a little noisemaker that Minh is using as a phone.

It's time to go back to our own hotel. On the way over, there's a beggar boy *with both arms missing*. He looks at Minh and makes a *"yuck"* sound, follows us, staring at her with *a grossed out expression*, and even pretends to shiver in revulsion!?!? We get to the Rex and watch another elaborate wedding reception in the courtyard. We send out one last load of laundry.

Our last step is supposed to be accomplished tomorrow. We are to pick up Minh's visa at the U.S. Consulate at 4PM!

Friday, June 1

We meet up with the Williams after breakfast. We go for a long stroll. They have paperwork to do at Immigration. Back at the Rex we get a taxi and go to the War Crimes Museum, *and later wish we hadn't.*

*The War Crimes (or War Remnants) Museum (**Nha trung bay toi acchien tranh**) was once called "Museum of American War Crimes." That should have told us something right away. This is where the headquarters of the U.S. Information Services once was. In the courtyard outside rests rusting war trophies, including tanks, a helicopter, fighter jet, howitzers, bombshells, even a guillotine that harvested heads at the Central Prison on **Ly Tu Trong**, first for the French, and later for Diem.*

*This museum reveals the manipulative language of propaganda. The main focus remains on atrocities committed by U.S. forces and their South Vietnamese allies. There are horrifying photos of destruction, paintings of barbaric treatments/torture carried out at **Con Son Prison**, and photos revealing massacre—the horrors that took place at **My Lai**, and unnerving graphics of victims of Napalm and white-phosphorous bombs.*

One entire room is devoted to the environmental ravages wrought by defoliants such as Agent Orange. There's a "Hostile Forces Room" which recounts backgrounds, actions, and fates of reactionary forces in the South post-1975. Two rooms are devoted to weapons. Out back is a replica "tiger cage," the pigsty-style prison cell used on Con Son Island.

The souvenir shop outside sells U.S. Army-issue fungicidal foot powder and dog tags, and models crafted from spent bullets. This is one excursion I could have done without. We keep Minh turned away from the displays, with an exciting toy to keep her attention. **We leave feeling rather queasy.**

We taxi back for lunch and nap time. *We leave the television on because she loves those sing-song cartoons that play midday.* Jimmy works out and spends time in the sauna while she sleeps.

We excitedly head to the U.S. Consulate for our 4PM appointment. We don't have to wait long before our names are called. We receive the visa, no problem! We go right to the Continental and let Minh and Trayton play. We all eat at the contemporary little corner café for lunch. We order desserts, mostly ice cream. *I order a cold banana split, I think. They bring out hot banana flambe. It's good even though I didn't order it.*

We talk with an American woman. We've seen her every morning at the Rex at breakfast. She has an older girl and a 2 year-old Vietnamese girl. *She tells us that her paperwork is messed up and she has now been here for 52 days! She's going crazy!* The 2 year-old is precious! She can't bear to take her back to the orphanage so she's been playing the dreaded bureaucracy waiting game. A lawyer is now trying to sort and straighten things out!?!?

We come back to our hotel around 7PM. We try to fit all of the stuff we've bought over the last 2 weeks in our suitcase somehow. *We brought an empty duffel bag just for this reason.* While in the lobby, a distraught Vietnamese man asks if we're adopting. We answer yes. **He offers us his 3 children**, who are standing behind him all clean and dressed up. He says his wife died and he can't continue to keep them. *We shake our heads no, that we just can't.* He then begs us to at least take the oldest girl and give her a good life. He doesn't want any money. He's just doing what he thinks would be best for his children. *The children hear all of this. It's so sad.* The same children are offered to the Williams when they come to the lobby. I guess they're just hanging out in the lobby since this hotel is a favorite of Americans and Europeans.

We spend the rest of the night packing, looking, and thinking about how much adventure we crammed into the past two weeks.

Saturday, June 2

We talk with the Williams, hug good-bye, and promise to visit and email before going to the airport with all of our bags, souvenirs, stroller…*We get through all of the security measures and checkpoints.* They call our flight number and we begin the **first leg of our 24-hour journey**. Minh loves the plane, the buttons, the ear plugs, *and the food* of course. *We bring a huge supply of Pringles!*

We land in Bangkok and take a taxi back to the Rama Gardens Hotel. We spend the night and will endure that last long flight tomorrow.

Bringing Our Angel Home

We arrive at the Pittsburgh International Airport around 6PM on June 3. My mom, our children, and my friend, Joan, are standing eagerly at the gate. Everyone stares at each other while hugging. I introduce Minh to her new brothers and sister. She warms up pretty fast. *The children are trying to excitedly fill us in on these last two weeks, everybody talking at once!* The children end up taking turns carrying Minh to baggage claim and then to the car. **Mama, Daddy, what'd you bring me???** We get home to Cranberry and try to find the little presents we brought back for everybody. They all like their Vietnamese trinkets, especially the silk **ao dai** for Morgan, the snake wine for Caleb and Lucas, and the miniature cyclo for Max.

At home, we see that it's going to take a while for Minh to get used to the puppies. They'll stay in the garage or outside. We'll slowly introduce them. She sleeps on our bedroom floor. All of the children lie on the floor and watch some videos we brought back, *movies with little children singing and dancing to traditional Vietnamese songs.* Minh adores them and the other children like them because they're different. Grandmother goes back home the day after we return. *She'll need a few days of rest after these two weeks!*

Our first week back is a busy one! The children get out of school for the summer. We have several graduation parties to attend. They're a lot of fun and Minh gets to dress up and meet people. We go to church Sunday and Jimmy introduces her to the congregation. **"For this child we prayed…"**

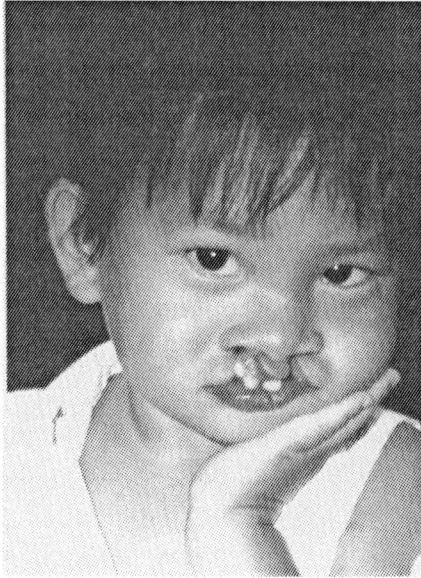

◆   ◆   ◆

The next couple of weeks are a time for adjustment and everyone finding *their new role and place in the family.* Minh goes to the pediatrician 5 days after we bring her home. She gets a thorough check-up and is found to be healthy under the circumstances. Her ears are infected. Dr. Lopez tries to get some of it out but it's dry and hard. She gives us drops to help soften it. Minh also has an all-over body rash so we're sent home with a body creme to apply. Because they don't really know the circumstances surrounding her immunizations, they begin them from the start. *She doesn't like that one bit, screams and kicks. I do too! HA!*

◆   ◆   ◆

Throughout the United States there are many qualified health professionals caring for children with cleft lip and palate. However, because these children frequently require a variety of services which need to be provided in a coordinated manner over a period of years, an interdisciplinary team is deemed the best route. The number of specialists on a team varies, but most crucial are an audiologist, a surgeon, a pediatric dentist, an orthodontist, a geneticist, a nurse, an otolaryngologist (ENT), a pediatrician, a psychologist, and a speech-language pathologist. **So, we search for a team because we want to find one before Minh arrives. We spend a lot of time on the internet. We call doctors and hospitals in Atlanta, Washington, D.C…and end up finding one of the best teams in the country right here in nearby Pittsburgh.** *We call and discuss Minh's situation with them and an appointment is set up before we even leave for Vietnam.*

The Cleft Palate-Craniofacial Center we choose is an interdisciplinary center located within the University of Pittsburgh School of Dental Medicine in Salk Hall. The center offers expertise and services for a broad range of birth defects. **They can be emailed at cleft@cpc.pitt.edu.**

◆   ◆   ◆

On June 20, we take her to the Cleft Palate-Craniofacial Center for her initial visit. First, we see an audiologist. Through many tests, they discover she has a substantial hearing loss. Her ears are also still impacted with wax and infection.

Children with clefts of the palate have an increased risk of ear infections. These problems are the result of inadequate function of some of the palatal muscles, which open the Eustachian tubes, "the small tubes connecting the throat to the middle ear." When the Eustachian tubes don't open effectively, air can't enter the middle ear. This lack of ventilation causes fluid to form and eventually accumulate in the middle ear. This condition is called **otitis media**. *The fluid can then become infected, causing the child to experience a fever and painful earache.*

Because of problems with ear infections, children with clefts of the palate may experience some hearing loss which changes over time. Audiologists can test even the youngest of infants, even newborns. For Minh, they perform testing called behavioral audiometry. She is set on my lap in a quiet, sound-treated room. Sounds are fed into the room through speakers, and her response to sound is observed by the audiologist. Responses like turning toward the source of the sound (localization) make it obvious when Minh hears the sound. The audiologist also uses toys that light up when she localizes the sound correctly.

Because of the frequency of this problem, children with clefts may require a minor surgical procedure called a **myringotomy***. This procedure consists of making a small slit in the eardrum to drain the fluid. Following drainage, tiny tubes are inserted in the slits to allow air to enter the middle air and prevent fluid from reforming. Once the tubes are out, these small slits heal readily and don't usually result in any permanent damage to the eardrum. Hopefully, this procedure can correct a major portion of Minh's hearing problems.*

Next we go to Tom's office. He's a very kind, knowledgeable nurse practitioner. He notes her weight, height…We explain how we use a straw or medicine dropper to feed her formula, any liquid. He gives us the idea of using a sippy cup that we've rigged. She can't suck but the cup works great when the bladder or *sucking apparatus* is removed. *It sure beats feeding her drop by excruciatingly slow drop!*

Our last stop at the Cleft Palate-Craniofacial Center is to see the plastic surgeon, Dr. Hurwitz. We research and pick him from many. *He's supposed to be the best around.* The doctor studies her face, takes digital pictures, calls colleagues for input…to plan the best possible route to take for *fixing* Minh. He has done countless cleft lip/palate repair operations but mostly on infants. Things are different with a 2 year-old. The tissue isn't as pliable, habits have developed, teeth are coming in…He's a very dedicated, sincerely caring man. *Minh slowly wins his heart just like she does with everyone she meets.* He plans her first surgery for the next month.

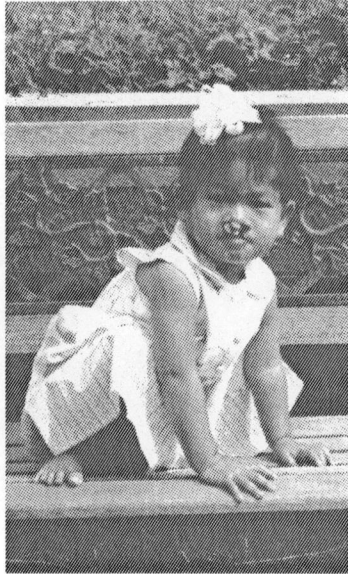

◆   ◆   ◆

With all of these appointments, Minh notices that her mouth and nose area do look a little different. She starts spending more time looking at her face and touching her teeth. *She finds some plastic vampire teeth left over from Halloween in the toy box and wears them around the house occasionally!?!? She also puts on her sister's orthodontic bands.* Minh comes up to me one day and I notice something on her front teeth. I look closer and see that she has taken Morgan's little orthodontic rubber bands and slipped them on her protruding front teeth.

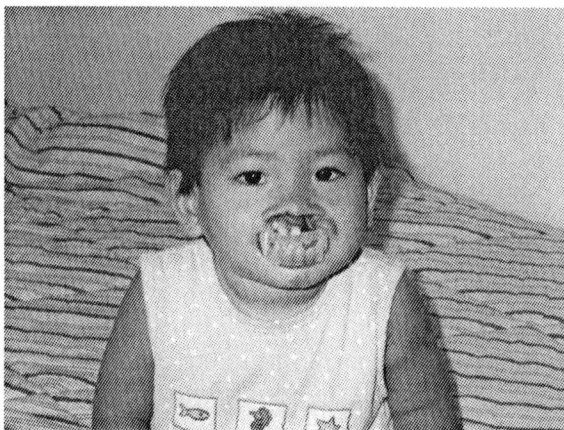

Shirley, our adoption case worker, comes to visit June 25. She's surprised at how well Minh has adapted. *It's as if Minh has always been a part of our family.* The only transition difficulty is between she and Max. They're both vying for that baby, or youngest, role in the family. They'll work it out when they see there is plenty of love, *food,* and time for everybody!

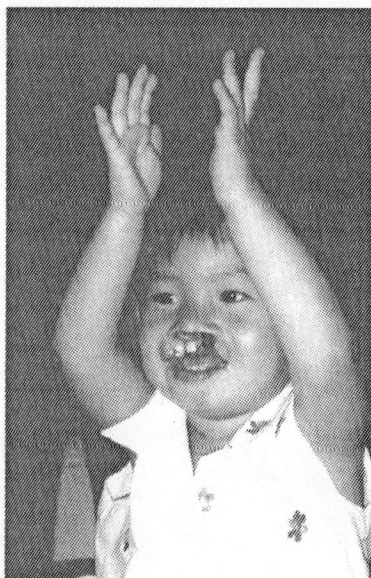

We go on with life as usual, *well usual for us*. We go camping, swimming, and on several other trips we had already planned. People are curious about Minh and we don't mind answering their questions. *She just flashes those big grins of hers!* On July 2, we go to Montefaire Hospital to see a prosthodontist that Dr. Hurwitz arranges for us to meet. *This woman's office has before/after pictures and samples of appliances she has made, including a prosthetic ear, nose , half of a skull…It's kind of like touring a Ripley's Believe It Or Not museum. It's amazing what modern medicine and technology can do these days!* Dr. Huber doesn't think Minh is a candidate for her services at this time. We go back to the Cleft Palate-Craniofacial Center July 10 to see an ENT. She agrees that Minh needs ear tubes so she plans to coordinate and do this short procedure during Dr. Hurwitz's first surgery, while Minh is already anesthetized. The audiologist performs more tests, too.

◆   ◆   ◆

The big day has come, July 18! Minh will have her first operation today. Dr. Hurwitz will do the lip repair and the ENT the myringotomy. *The lip repair is a surgical closure of the lip which **usually** occurs after an infant has demonstrated steady weight gain, around 3-4 months of age. The objective of surgery on the lip is to close the cleft so that scarring will be minimal, the appearance is normal, and the face develops normally.* We take Minh to Children's Hospital in Pittsburgh at 7AM. She's changed into little hospital pajamas and we're taken to the operating holding room. Dr. Hurwitz explains his intended procedure to us again and we sign all releases. Minh is running around playing with the toys, *not a care in the world*. The anesthesiologist comes over, **lets us kiss her good-bye**, and carries her to the operating room. *Minh holds her arms out to us, screaming and staring at us with wild eyes.* She doesn't understand why we've handed her off to a stranger. *I've tried to explain but how much can a 2 year-old understand?* I calm down and wait. Jimmy waits for a while but has to go back to work.

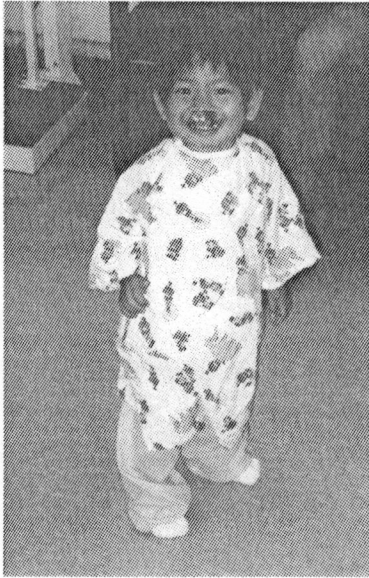

A couple of hours later, Dr. Hurwitz comes out to tell me the surgery went fine. He tries to prepare me by revealing that her nose is flat and there's a lot of swelling right now. The main thing, though, is that she has lips and he didn't damage any of her baby (or permanent) teeth in the process. He explains that he'll want to wait and do the palate surgery in 7-8 months, giving her mouth plenty of time to heal.

A nurse takes me back to the recovery room. I sit in a rocking chair and they put **a swaddled Minh** in my arms. *Truthfully, I'm alarmed at first. Her nose is pulled down tight and her lips are huge and swollen. She looks like a baby tiger cub!?!?* **I miss my baby's happy, goofy face!** *Am I crazy!? She's softly crying, not moving her mouth, but letting the tears well up and roll down her cheeks.* There's dried blood caked in her hair and nose. I just look, pray, and keep telling myself that we've done the right thing and everything will come out okay.

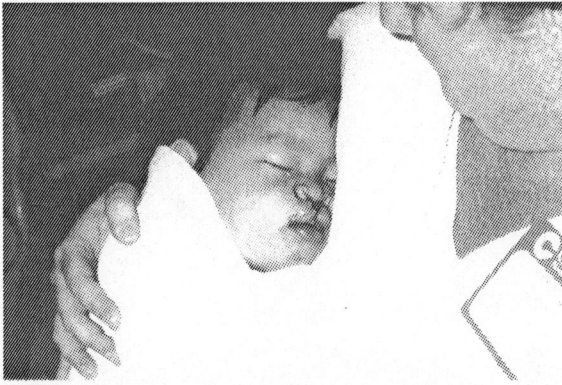

We're taken to our room and she won't let me put her down or anyone else hold her. I cuddle her and she starts spitting up blood and crying. The nurses say this is normal and gives me a small basin and some tissues. The staff at Children's is great but parents have to do a lot themselves because the sick children don't want nurses touching them. *I know Minh doesn't want any staff getting near.* I had told Jimmy to go on back to work, that I could handle things, and he could come by later after he checked on our children. **Things change!** I need him now. *He's so much better with blood and guts. I wanted to be the one to stay with her because I'm much better at cuddling. We need a blood person right now, though.* I call his office, our home, his cell phone, even a friend of ours to find him. I tell him to come as soon as possible.

Jimmy speeds thinking something is wrong. Things are calm by the time he gets there. I've calmed but my white shirt is covered with blood where she threw up on me and more on my chest where she's been drooling on it. He holds her while I clean up and change. He tells me that her swelling will go down and every day that area will transform, get better. *I know and have been told all of that but need to be reassured.* He leaves to care for our children and I prepare to stay the night.

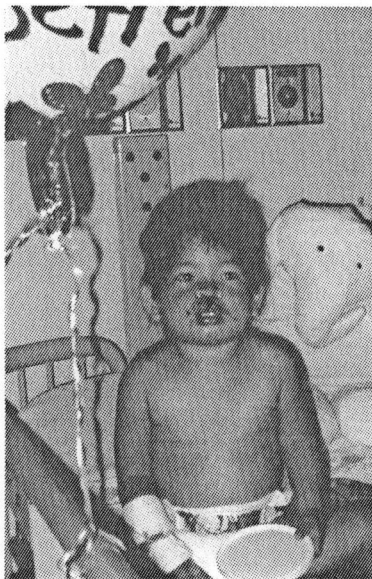

She sleeps and I get a basin of warm water and clean her up. She actually likes the feel of the warm cloth and is very soothed by her sponge bath. The nurse also brings in ointment and hydrogen peroxide for her lip area. With these, I clean the blood from her nose and apply ointment to her dry, split lips. ***I put her snazzy pink leopard pajamas on and she feels much better!*** I hold her for hours and finally put her in the crib late that night. The nurses come and go all night taking her vital signs (temperature, blood pressure, check the IV drip..). She screams and holds her arms out for me to pick her up each time they enter the room. She really gets no sleep.

The next morning she won't drink or eat. They bring broth, jello…I finally get some *Fruit Loops* from the nearby pantry which she sticks one by one in the back of her mouth and chews slowly with her back teeth. Later on, she lets me feed her some lemon ice. She sleeps a lot in the morning. Jimmy comes to get us and we leave that afternoon. We pick up our children at Joan's house. Morgan and Max are a little taken back when they see her. They just hurry and get in the car.

Jimmy tells them the swelling will go down...*Caleb and Lucas say she looks like a cat and teach her to meow!?!? **BOYS!!!***

We stay at home through the weekend. She gets better each day and is eating and running around wild again in no time. *Life gets back on track, everyone busy with normal summer stuff.* A few days after her surgery, we take her to Dr. Hurwitz's private office for a follow-up appointment. She's recovering nicely, still a little red under her nose but that should clear up soon. There are numerous stitches inside her nose and mouth that will eventually dissolve or work their way out. That accounts for some of the redness. We keep *doctoring her up* with antibiotic ointment and hydrogen peroxide. ***I take a photo just these 4 short days after her operation and the transformation is already miraculous!*** We take her for another round of immunizations 4 days later. *Needless to say, the closer we now get to anything that resembles a doctor's office, the more agitated she becomes. I would, too.* The pediatrician is amazed at the results of her lip repair. *She says it's healing great!*

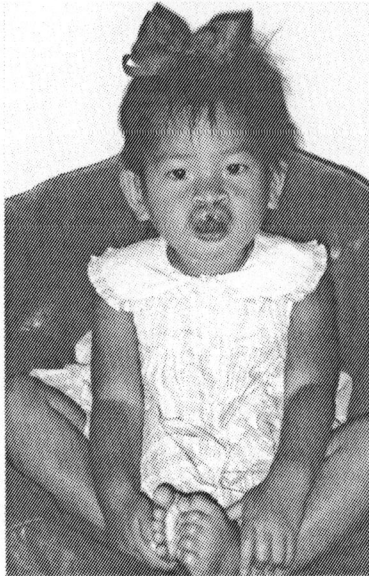

◆   ◆   ◆

It's toward the end of summer vacation so we make plans for a **Road Trip**! Jimmy can't get off work right now for that many days so I map out our itinerary using *the convenient Yahoo directions.* The day after her immunizations, the five children and I hop in our big van and head down south. *Jimmy just waves good-bye, shaking his head!?!?* So, July 28, we drive to Murfreesboro, Tennessee and visit with my younger sister and her family. My mom flies down from Chicago and my older sister and her children drive up from Atlanta for the week, too. We swim, shop, eat, play, *give every one a chance to get to know Minh.*

On August 4, we pack up and drive west to Humboldt, Tennessee. There, we visit my in-laws and big brother's family. Jimmy's little brother and his family come from Memphis, too. **Minh quickly endears herself to each and every family member.** While in Humboldt, part of her lip gets infected and swells so I call Dr. Hurwitz and he calls in a strong oral antibiotic. *I take a photo for documentation purposes in case he needs it upon our return.* He also suggests using warm compresses to bring the rest of the infection out. It takes a few days but this regimen works fine.

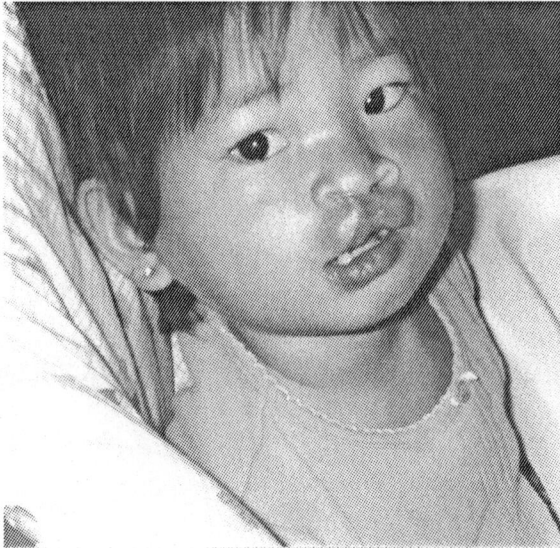

After spending time there, we drive back home to Cranberry Penn-sylvania, *visiting interesting places and fun things all along the way.* We call Jimmy every night to tell him where we are. We have to listen to the *"be careful, stay in well-populated hotels, don't stay on the first floor, don't stay out late in unfamiliar cities..speech."* He really misses us and we're ready to get home. We arrive August 11 in time to pack Caleb and Lucas off to summer Church Camp for a few days, enjoy a family weekend at *Hershey Park and Chocolate World*, and the start of the 2001-2002 school year.

◆   ◆   ◆

Well, ***just like every American***, September brought unexpected twists and turns. Jimmy receives military orders soon after the 9/11 mayhem. *We're moving to Montana, SOON! We make moving plans and start preparing the children, positively, for our next adventure.* We promptly call Dr. Hurwitz. We admire and trust him so much that we prefer he do Minh's crucial palate operation if at all possible. We talk and discuss and talk and discuss. He agrees to move her surgery from

February 2002, up to October 2001! My mom and Tony come up for the last weekend in September, primarily to spend time with Minh before this next major operation.

October is a whirlwind of activity! We go to Court on October 1 where Minh's foreign adoption is made final in the U.S. and her name is **legally changed from *Pham Tam Minh* to *Gracie Minh Pillow*!** She's a little confused as Jimmy leads her up to the big courthouse. She trusts him now, though, so she's not frightened. I think she understands what the judge and lawyers are saying. She smiles at us and pats our hands. **She's not only emotionally bonded with us now, but forever legally attached as well.**

◆   ◆   ◆

We're informed the very next day that Minh has been carved out some operating room time for the next day! *Can we bring her in at 7AM tomorrow, October 3!?!?* Of course we agree and make the necessary arrangements. *Whew! A palate repair is when the surgeon closes the palate, **usually occurring** between 8-18months of age.*

The palate is the roof of the mouth. The front part contains bone and is hard (hard palate). The back part doesn't contain bone and is soft (soft palate). A cleft palate is an opening in the roof of the mouth. A cleft palate doesn't mean that the palate is "missing" although it may look that way. It means that the two sides of the palate didn't fuse as the unborn baby was developing. Cleft palates can vary in extent. Minh's case is severe. An incomplete cleft palate involves the back of the soft palate, while a complete cleft palate extends the length of the palate to just behind the gums. Minh's is complete, with just a gaping space. Because the lip and palate develop separately, it's possible for a child to have only a cleft lip, only a cleft palate, or both.

A major goal of palatal surgery is to ensure good speech quality at the earliest age. Children with clefts of the palate tend to develop speech and language a bit more slowly than other children. Without a palate, only 4 different sounds can be uttered, so for most, forming consonant sounds is out of the question. Children may or may not sound normal before palatal surgery is performed, but they tend to "catch up" afterward. This "catch up" process often continues for four or five years. Approximately 80% of children with a cleft of the palate develop normal speech once their palates are closed. Many of these children require speech therapy.

We bring her to Children's Hospital where she's again given some cute little pediatric pajamas. This time, the anesthesiologist gives her a small cup of something designed to calm her down, take away the fears, and prepare her for surgery. We're then taken to the surgical holding bay. **That medicine kicks in!** *Minh can't hardly hold her head up, happy but drunk and with no inhibitions. HA!* **Jimmy is holding her and she's holding a toy microphone singing like a lounge singer, like a tipsy and slightly lethargic lounge singer!** *Her head bobs back and forth while she smiles and belts out her slurry songs!* We laugh and laugh!

Dr. Hurwitz comes in to go over the details of this morning's surgery. He'll repair her palate and also create a **pharyngeal flap**. This surgery will take several hours and is much more complicated. She doesn't cry this time when she's carried back for surgery. The hours tick by. Jimmy and I wait and wait. Dr. Hurwitz comes out to tell us that the surgery was a success. She'll stay in the hospital for a few days to make sure the flap isn't too large and/or doesn't cause breathing problems.

When a child can't achieve velopharyngeal closure, this pharyngoplasty procedure is needed. **Velopharyngeal closure** *is the closing of the nasal cavity from the oral cavity which directs air used in speech through the mouth rather than the nose. It requires interaction of the muscles in the* *palate and the back of the throat. The ability to create closure is necessary for good speech.*

We go to the recovery room and hold her. *She's not a happy camper! She doesn't scream but uncomfortably squirms and cries.* **She's so pale!** The surgeon explains that she lost a lot of blood and a blood transfusion may be needed. They get us a room and we settle in. Jimmy's parents come the next day and stay through the weekend to help with the other children while Minh recovers. After a full day and night she's able to eat some ice cream. She's not able to eat any food but we find that she likes the taste of baby food. *She's not recovering as quickly but this surgery was much more extensive than the first.* She needs pain medication regularly, *morphine.* **She stays comfortably drug-induced for a couple of days.** Doug, a friend from church, visits and Minh recognizes him as a safe, familiar friend and seems to enjoy this respite. Her energy *and color* pick up and a blood transfusion thankfully isn't needed after all. On the last day, they start giving her Tylenol with Codeine.

We go home late October 5. *She sleeps soundly in her bed, not interrupted by nurses and late-night beeps and IV alarms sounding.* I still give her Tylenol regularly to keep her comfortable. By the weekend, she feels almost normal. We take her out to get fresh air and she enjoys our excursions to Amish Country and Traxx Farms to pick out Halloween pumpkins. Granny and Pops leave Monday, October 8.

◆   ◆   ◆

Again, life returns to *normal.* We take her to the Cleft Palate-Craniofacial Center October 17 for a routine visit. Her hearing has greatly improved since getting the ear tubes in July. *She helps me share information about Vietnam during a local school's Cultural Fair.*

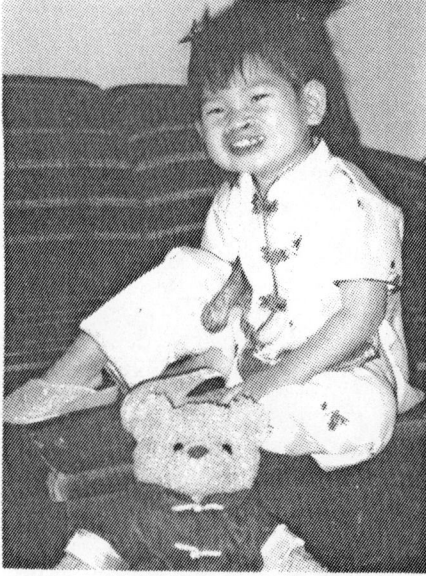

We *trick or treat* on Halloween and she tries to eat each piece of candy as she receives it. Minh can eat so much better after having the palate surgery. She's also experimenting more with sounds, trying to talk and form words. She's finally used to Skippy and Chiklet. She adores Chiklet, *hugging her tight,* kissing her all of the time. **They're best pals!**

November is even busier than October! Shirley comes for her final home visit. We try to make this *a good one* since this will be the last time we see her. Everyone is clean, changed into decent clothes, house is actually picked up, puppies are tucked away in the garage...*About 10 minutes before her arrival, the lights go out, not just our house, **a whole town black-out**!!!* We've already packed a lot of things preparing for our move to Montana, including the 80+ candles we own. Well, we find a few flashlights and borrow a couple of candles from neighbors. Shirley comes and does the whole process by candle light, *the children trying to touch the wax from the dripping candles, Max turning off and on the flashlight...!?!?*

◆   ◆   ◆

We spend the next couple of weeks saying our final good-byes and packing up all of the stuff we've accumulated over the last few years. *The good byes are the hardest we've ever experienced. We've become so much a part of this community that the parting is very painful, for all of us.*

Minh has an appointment for her last round of immunizations November 7 and a final visit to the Cleft Palate-Craniofacial Center on November 15. After she sees the plastic surgeon, audiologist, and nurse practitioner, she sees a speech/language pathologist. We decide that speech therapy isn't necessary in Minh's case. Right now, Jimmy and I have a program of speech and language stimulation. Of course, Minh having four siblings helps, too. They're always trying to teach her to say words and she's forever-ready to learn and try her best.

As far as dental care goes, it's coordinated among several dental specialists interacting on the team. Minh's cleft has affected the **alveolar ridge** *(the bony ridge of the maxilla and mandible containing the teeth). In the future, she may need to be fitted with speech appliances (***obturators***) or even prostheses until the surgeon connects her upper gum with* **bone graft surgery** *around her 7th or 8th birthday. The next step will be extensive orthodontics when she's older, after the gum is connected.*

Before surgery, the skin on both sides of Minh's philtral columns was unattached. It stuck straight out from her nose. The **philtral columns** *are normal ridges in the skin of the central upper lip connecting the peaks of the Cupid's bow to the back of the nose. The* **premaxilla** *is the small bone in the upper jaw which contains the upper four front teeth. Minh's premaxilla protruded quiet far. This is normally connected with the side segments of the upper jaw, but was and will remain separated in Minh's case until she's 7 or 8 years old.*

◆   ◆   ◆

We leave Pennsylvania November 20. We finish packing, load up a 24-foot moving truck that Jimmy drives pulling the Land Cruiser on a trailer, and I drive the van pulling a 12-foot trailer crammed with more stuff. The children take turns riding first with me, then with Jimmy in the truck…We drive down south for Thanksgiving. After the holidays, we strike out for **Big Sky Country**. We drive and visit friends and gawk at touristy items all along the way.

Our favorite stop on this wild west adventure is in Sioux Falls, SD where we visit the Williams. We even spend the night, talking and catching up. We get to South Dakota on the eve of their first huge snow! WOW! It's so good to see Dayton and Tracy, and especially little Trayton. He's as cute as ever! When he and Minh see each other, at first they cry and try to get away from each other. That's an unusual and unexpected response. We try and get them used to each other again. When they finally realize no one is being left or taken away, they revel in their reunion. **Minh immediately falls into that "big sister role" just like at the orphanage. They hug and babble. Minh shows him her mouth. He rubs her lips and stares at her. It's fascinating seeing them reconnect!** *Dayton and Tracy take us to their animal hospital early the next morning. We see Dayton hard at work. The children pet a snake named All-star, talk to birds, pester cats and dogs…*

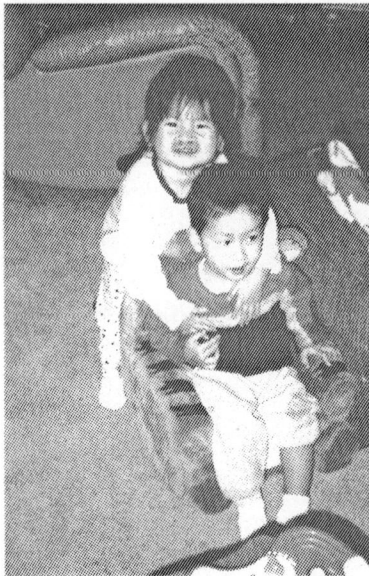

We travel through Kentucky, Illinois, Missouri, Iowa, Nebraska, South Dakota, Wyoming, and finally into Montana a week later. We stop and explore everything, **yes, everything**...from a Corn Palace in SD (*yes, an entire civic center made of corn art, A-MAIZE-ING!!!*)...travel through the Badlands and Yellowstone...drive up deserted, steep mountain roads with our entourage of vehicles to view magnificent Mount Rushmore...a stop in Sundance to see Billy the Kid's old stomping grounds and Devil's Tower in WY...walk the Cahokia Indian Mounds in IL...Jesse James' home in MO...Cowboy Alley and Silver Dollar Saloon in Wall, SD...the Little Bighorn and Custer Museum on the Crow Indian Reservation in MT...

◆   ◆   ◆

We're settled in now at our new home in Helena, Montana. *Again, life has returned to normal.* **What is OUR normal!?!?** I home-school the children here so they can spend more time on music, studying foreign languages, and traveling. We travel as much as possible. The children learn so much more by *experiences*, rather than reading about a topic in a book or watching videos. **I love Samuel Johnson's quote: "The use of travel is to regulate imagination by reality, and, instead of thinking how things may be, to see them as they are."** *Minh watches, copies, and learns massive amounts through example.* Minh will probably ultimately be quite gifted. She sits and listens while her brothers and sister are using computer programs or learning new facts through flash cards or discussion. *She gets a big box of crayons, climbs up in her booster chair, and thinks she's in school, too.*

She's scheduled for her first Cleft Lip/Palate appointment here in Helena on March 15. They'll schedule her third surgery for later this year. She has an abnormal opening (called a **fistula**) in her palate that needs to be repaired. Fistulas sometimes occur after especially-difficult palate surgeries. *The surgery will help improve her speech and alleviate some of the other **cool tricks** she has learned to perform!* One day she accidentally gets Cool Whip in the opening and it comes out her nose when she coughs. *The boys laugh and laugh!!!* She quickly realizes how easy it is to flick a bean up through the opening with her tongue and blow it our her nose. *Morgan tells her that it's gross! Caleb, Lucas, and Max, on the other hand, think it's the most awesome trick ever!* We scold her but the laughs that she gets override any punishments we could dole out. So, I'm pretty anxious for this next surgery to be scheduled. ***We've now seen bits of Vienna sausages, pie meringue, and a baked bean fly out of her nose, amid peals of laughter and misguided encouragement!***

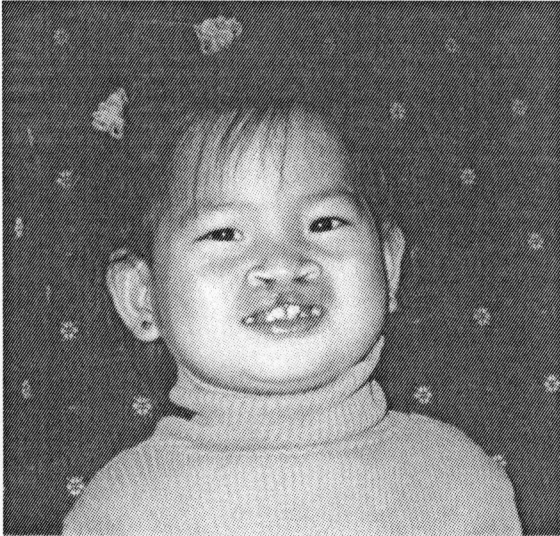

◆   ◆   ◆

Minh continues to be an absolute joy. She has such a fun, nurturing personality! **Since her surgeries, it's simply amazing to watch her stare at herself in the mirror...touching her new face and smacking her plushy, pretty lips created in the first surgery. She loves to pucker up those new lips and kiss everybody...*she uses her tongue too when kissing but we're working on that!?!?* She's an angel, a feisty one, but definitely a little miracle. She flourishes with all of the attention and adventure!

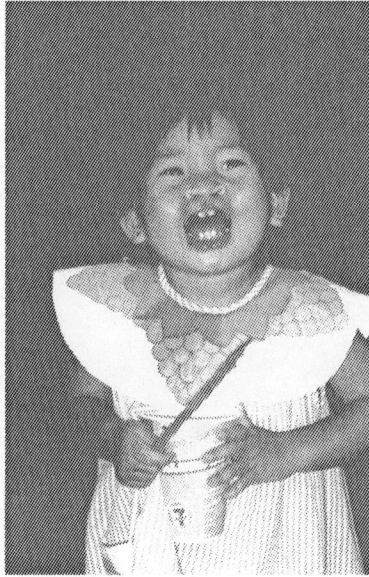

Speaking of adventure, we're now preparing for our next one! Jimmy has taken off a couple of weeks in February. We live close to a major Space-A terminal, McChord Air Force Base in Washington. *For those non-military readers*, Space-A is a program for military and his/her dependents. We can fly on military aircraft for free on any open/available seats. The planes from McChord fly missions all over the world, *more regularly to Alaska, Guam, Australia, Japan, Hawaii, Tutuilla Island (American Samoa), New Zealand, Korea...*mostly Pacific destinations.

As part of our home-school work, the children all applied for and received passports. We've researched the climates of all possible destinations and singled out the warm-weather ones *(leaves out Alaska, Japan, and Korea—in February)*. We'll each pack a book bag of shorts, swimsuits...and drive to McChord AFB February 8. We'll fly on the first plane available that has 7 open seats, *as long as it's going somewhere warm*. Minh's assignment *before departure* is to get completely potty-trained, *no extra room for diapers, wipes...*She's wearing tiny panties for the 4th consecutive day now. *She's doing exceptionally well!* **We'll** research *where we've been* and *what we've seen* when we return from *wherever...*

Wish us luck!

Epilogue

About a month after we return with Gracie Minh, we receive letters from Holt. The first is a letter to us *(the new parents)* from Holt's President and CEO, Dr. John Williams. It's a note offering his hearty congratulations on Minh's new place in our family and relaying the post-adoption services available, *if needed*, in the years ahead. He writes: ***"Our hearts are full as we think of the love that is filling your lives and the belonging that the precious child has found in your family."***

◆   ◆   ◆

He also encloses a letter and photo *(of Bertha or **Grandma Holt** as she's called)* for Minh. This expression of caring will I know someday *when she's older* be such a blessing! **It's so special that I'm including it in its entirety:**

Dear Minh,

I want to welcome you home to your family. You have made the monumental journey from your birth country into a new life–into your new family where you will be loved and belong.

I want you to know that we at Holt International will also and always consider you a member of the "Holt" family. You are a part of the adoptive families and adoptees, birth parents, donors, staff and volunteers who care deeply for children like you. You have a special place in our hearts, and we hope to stay in touch with you throughout your journeys.

Our founder, "Grandma" Bertha Holt who passed away recently, used to send a letter to all newly arrived children. In this letter she expressed much of what is in our hearts as we celebrate your arrival home. She wrote:

149

I'll always be interested in knowing and hearing about all the exciting things that are filling your life. I pray that you will be blessed with joy and be a source of great happiness for your family. Remember that you are unique and there is no one in the world quite like you. My prayer for you is that you will grow and learn to your fullest potential and to know the Lord as your Savior.

Though you may have grandparents through your new family, I hope you will think of Bertha Holt as your own special "Grandma." She and her husband pioneeered international adoption and proved that a family's love can transcend all boundaries. Grandma helped lay much of the groundwork for adoption around the world today.

We surely enjoy the privilege of having a part in your life.

Yours,
Dr. John L. Williams

Afterword

about **<u>Holt International Children's Services</u>**

If you or someone you know is thinking about adoption, *or has a heart for helping the many little displaced ones around the world*, I urge you to give Holt a look. For information, go online at www.holt-intl.org.

Holt maintains this website with up-to-date information about all of its programs. They have an extensive list of recommended books, helpful forums, the *HiFamiles* magazine, and information on how you can help other homeless children through the **Sponsorship** program, **Planned Giving**, and through the **Adoption Fund for Children with Special Needs**.

(I know some of these efforts benefitted Gracie Minh only indirectly, but without them, I would probably not be holding her in my arms today.)

about **<u>Cleft Lip and/or Palate</u>**

If you have a baby born with this birth defect or choose to adopt a baby or older child with cleft lip and/or palate, please simply take it day by day. Know that even ***imperfect angels*** have big missions here on Earth. You've been sent a gift, ***a wee celestial presence from above***, to impart lessons of humility, compassion, predilection, and grace. Love this pure, lively soul and you'll be rewarded a thousand times over.

There are countless websites, publications, and professionals to talk to concerning cleft lip and/or palate. The organizations I suggest starting with are **WIDE SMILES** (www.widesmiles.org), the **CLEFT PALATE FOUNDATION** (www.cleft.com) and **ABOUT FACE** out of Canada (www.aboutfaceinternational.com).

About the Author

Tracy S. Pillow currently lives in beautiful Helena, Montana with her soldier husband, five energetic kids, and spoiled puppy named Chiklet. She volunteers for Holt International Children's Services, writes and photographs for several publications, represents an international exchange program (Center for Cultural Interchange), and homeschools the brood—in between cooking, playing, cleaning, traveling, *and yes*, occasionally sleeping.

Glossary

All Vietnamese words are italicized.

adopt—to choose or take as one's own

Agent Orange—defoliant herbicide used to deprive guerrillas of forest cover

ala—wing-like part or expansion of a bone

alveolar ridge—the bony ridge of the **maxilla** and mandible containing the teeth

Animism—the belief that natural objects, natural phenomena, and the universe itself possess souls

ao dai—traditional dress of Vietnamese women/girls, comprising baggy pants and a long, slit tunic

audiologist—a person with a degree, license, and certification in audiology (science of hearing) who measures hearing, identifies hearing loss, and participates in rehabilitation of hearing impairment

authenticate—to establish as genuine

Bach Ding—White Villa

baht—monetary units used in **Thailand**

Bangkok—a seaport in and the capital of **Thailand**, in the south-central part, on the Chao Phraya

Bao Tang Lich Su Viet Nam—Vietnam Museum of History

Ben Ter.—one of the Vietnamese **provinces**

bilateral—pertaining to, involving, or affecting two or both sides

Binh Duong—one of Vietnam's southern **provinces**

Buddhism—a religion, originated in India by Buddha and later spreading to China, Burma, Japan, Tibet, and parts of SE Asia, holding that life is full of suffering caused by desire and that the way to end this suffering is through enlightenment that enables one to halt the endless sequence of births and deaths to which one is otherwise subject

buncha—rice noodles with barbecued pork

Buu Dien—Municipal Post Office

Cambodia—a republic in SE Asia, formerly part of French **Indochina**; Phnom Penh, capital

Cao Dai Holy See—temple where the followers of **Cao Daism** worship

Cao Daism—indigenous religion, essentially a hybrid of **Buddhism**, **Taoism**, **Confucianism**, but hinged around an attempt at unification of all earthly codes of belief

cha gio—southern word for spring roll

Champa—Indianized Hindu empire that held sway in much of the southern half of Vietnam until the late 17th century

cheo—traditional folk opera

Chitrlada—palace of Thailand's royal family

Cholon—Vietnam's Chinatown, means "big market"

chu nom—classic Vietnamese script, based upon Chinese

cleft lip—a **congenital** deformed lip, usually the upper one, in which there is a vertical fissure, causing it to resemble the cleft lip of a hare, thus the name harelip

cleft palate—a **congenital** defect of the palate in which a longitudinal fissure exists in the roof of the mouth

Communism—a social and economic system in which property and goods are owned by the government and are to be shared equally by all the people

Confucianism—the system of ethics, education, and statesmanship taught by Confucius and his disciples, stressing love for humanity, ancestor worship, reverence for parents, and harmony in thought and conduct

congenital—a disease, deformity, or deficiency existing at the time of birth

con khi—monkey

con trau—buffalo

coolie hat—a wide, conical straw hat worn mostly as a shield against the sun

craniofacial anomaly—a visible, structural and /or functional difference affecting the head (cranium) and /or face

***Cu Chi* tunnels**—underground village used during past wars, as early as 1948

Cuu Long—means Nine Dragons, the 9 provinces of the Mekong Delta area

cyclo—three-wheeled bicycle with a carriage on the front

dan ball—a musical instrument made from a dried gourd, stick, and long copper wire

dat nuoc—word for "country" which literally translates as "land-water"

debride—to thoroughly clean a wound

defoliate—to destroy or cause widespread loss of leaves in (an area of jungle, forest, etc.), as by using chemical sprays or incendiary bombs, in order to deprive enemy troops or guerrilla forces of concealment

deforest—to divest or clear of forest or trees

delta—an area of land at the mouth of a river, is formed by deposits of mud, sand, and pebbles, often shaped like a triangle—"The word **delta** comes from the 4th letter in the Greek alphabet. The letter delta was drawn as a triangle, and the deltas in rivers are often in the shape of a triangle."

doi moi—free-market policy, Vietnam's economic restructuring

dong—Vietnamese monetary unit of money

dossier—a collection or file of documents containing detailed information about a person

durian—*(sau rieng)* fruit of a tree, of the bombax family, having a hard, prickly rind, a highly flavored, pulpy flesh, and an unpleasant odor

elephant ear fish—*(ca tai tuong)*, a local speciality, as large as a dinner plate, wrapped in rice paper and dipped in sauce

Eustachian tubes—tubes connecting the throat to the middle ear

flambe—dessert served in flaming liquor, mostly brandy

fistula—an abnormal opening

gecko—small, mostly nocturnal tropical lizards, having toe pads that can cling to smooth surfaces

guava—*(oi)*, a fruit with granular pink flesh encased in a thick green pear-shaped skin

hai—beaded velvet slippers that curve up at the toe

Hanoi—the capital of **Vietnam**, in the northern part on the Songka River

hat—singing

HiFamilies—bimonthly magazine published by Holt International Children's Services

Hoa—ethnic Chinese

hoa lan—orchid

Ho Chi Minh City—largest city and seaport in southern Vietnam, formerly **Saigon**

homestudy—process of compiling documentation, home visits by a Social Worker, education and preparation of the adoptive family, culminating in the Social Worker's summary and recommendation

Indochina—the region of Asia comprising **Vietnam**, **Laos**, and **Cambodia**

Jade Emperor—key figure in Vietnamese worship

khan dong—traditional hat worn by children and adults

Khmer—ethnic Cambodian

Kinh—ethnic Vietnamese

Lang Ca Dng—Whale Temple

Laos—a country in SE Asia, formerly part of French **Indochina**; Vientiane, capital

longan—*(nhan)*, a fruit with smooth, light brown skin and inside a translucent white pulp encasing a large, black seed

lychee—*(vai)*, fruit with dark red, bumpy skin

maxilla—the upper jaw

montagnards—French term for Vietnam's ethnic minority people

myringotomy—a minor surgical procedure in which a small slit is made in the eardrum to allow fluid to drain from the middle ear

My Tho—southern Mekong Delta town

napalm—jellied fuel dropped by U.S. forces during the Vietnam/American War, and capable of causing terrible burns

Nha Tho Duc Ba—Notre Dame Cathedral

Nha Trung Bay Toi Acchien Tranh—War Crimes Museum

Nui Ba Den—Black Lady Mountain

nuoc cham—fish sauce

nuoc dua—coconut juice

obturate—to stop up, close

Oc Eo—ancient seaport of the Funan Empire, east of modern-day Rach Gia in the Mekong Delta

On Dao Dua—Coconut Monk

orthodontics—the speciality of dentistry concerned with the correction and prevention of irregularities and malocclusion of the teeth and jaws

otalaryngologist—an "ear, nose, and throat" physician specializing in the diagnosis and management of head and neck disorders

otitis media—inflammation of the middle ear with accumulation of thick, mucous-like fluid

paddy—unharvested rice

pagoda—Buddhist place of worship

palate—the roof of the mouth including the front portion, or hard palate, and the back portion, or soft palate (also called the velum)

pediatrician—physician specializing in treatment of children

pharyngeal—of, pertaining to, or situated near the pharynx

philtral columns—normal ridges in the skin of the central upper lip connecting the peaks of the Cupid's bow to the back of the nose

pho—hot soup made with rice noodles

Phra Pathom Chedi—world's tallest Buddhist **stupa**

Phuoc Hai—Emperor Jade Pagoda

Phuong Island—island in the Mekong, home to an offbeat religious sect

premaxilla—the small bone in the upper jaw which contains the upper four front teeth

propaganda—information or ideas that are deliberately spread to try to influence the thinking of others, often not completely true or fair

prosthodontist—a dentist who specializes in providing prosthetic appliances for oral structures

province—an administrative division or unit of a country

quoc ngu—the modern, official writing system, using small lines or other symbols above or next to the letters indicating their tone

rambutan—*(chom chom)* bright red oval fruit of a Malayan, sapindaceous tree, covered with soft spines, or hairs, and having a subacid taste

R & R—means "rest and relaxation," term coined during the Vietnam/American War to describe a soldier's temporary leave of duty

Saigon—former name of **Ho Chi Minh City**, capital of former South Vietnam 1954-1976

sampan—flat-bottomed cargo boat

son mai—lacquerware

speech-language pathologist—an individual with the necessary academic training and experience to be certified or licensed to diagnose and treat disorders of speech, language, and communication

stupa—monumental pile of earth or other material, in memory of Buddha or a Buddhist saint, and commemorating some event or marking a sacred spot

Ta-laat Tay-wait—Bangkok's Thewes Flower Market

Taoism—the philosophical system evolved by Lao-tzu and Chuang-tzu, advocating a life of complete simplicity and naturalness and of noninterference with the course of natural events, in order to attain a happy existence in harmony with the Tao

Tay Ninh—south Vietnamese city, home of **Cao Dai Holy See**

Tet—the Vietnamese New Year celebration

Tet Offensive—an offensive by **Viet Cong** and North Vietnamese forces against South Vietnamese and U.S. positions in South Vietnam, beginning on Jan. 31, 1968, the start of **Tet**

Thailand—formerly Siam, a kingdom in SE Asia; **Bangkok**, capital

Thanh Hoang—Ruler of Hell

Thien Hau—Chinese pagoda in **Cholon**

thit—meat; *cay* or *cho*, dog; *con ran*, snake; *rua*, turtle; *nhim*, porcupine

to rung—stone xylophone

tunnel rats—American soldiers trained for warfare in tunnels such as those at Cu Chi

unilateral—relating to, occurring on, or involving one side only

VC *(Viet Cong)*—literally "Vietnamese Communists," used to describe the guerrilla

velopharyngeal closure—the closing of the nasal cavity from the oral cavity which directs the air used in speech through the mouth rather than the nose, requires interaction of the muscles in the palate and the back of the throat

vermilion—red portion, as of the lips

Vietnam—official name Socialist Republic of Vietnam, a country in SE Asia, comprising the former states of Annam, Tonkin, and Cochin-China; formerly part of French **Indochina**; divided into North Vietnam and South Vietnam during the Vietnam War but now reunified; **Hanoi**, capital

Vietnam War—a conflict, starting in 1954 and ending in 1975, between South Vietnam (later aided by the U.S., South Korea, Australia, the Philippines, Thailand, and New Zealand) and the **Viet Cong** and North Vietnam

viperine—or called snake wine or snake liquor, *ruou ran*

visa—a stamp in your passport giving you permission to enter and exit a country

wat—in **Thailand**, a Buddhist temple

Wat Benchamobophit—the Marble Wat

Wat Po—Temple of the Reclining Buddha

Wat Trimit—the Golden Buddha temple

Bibliography

BOOKS:

Adoption Process Guidebook: Vietnam (Holt International Children's Services)

Compact World Atlas (Dorling Kindersley Limited)

Discovery Channel's Insight Pocket Guide: Bangkok (by Steve Van Beek, updated by Lance Woodruff)

Discovery Channel's Insight Pocket Guide: Vietnam (by Lucy Forwood; APA Publications)

Fodor's Exploring Vietnam (by Fiona Dunlop)

Fodor's Southeast Asia (Fodor's Travel Publications, Inc.)

Frommer's Southeast Asia (by Jennifer Eveland, Michelle Fama, Mary Herczog, Stacy Lu, Beth Reiber, and Jon Sisken)

Lonely Planet's Travel Survival Kit: Vietnam (Lonely Planet Publications)

MacMillan Dictionary for Children (Simon and Schuster)

The Rough Guide to Vietnam (by Jan Dodd and Mark Lewis)

Traveler's Guide to Asian Customs and Manners (by Elizabeth Devine and Nancy Braganti)

Vietnam (by Jacques Nepote and Xavier Guillaume; Odyssey Publications, Ltd.)

<u>**Webster's Unabridged Dictionary of the English Language**</u> (RHR Press)

WEBSITES:

About Face (<u>www.aboutfaceinternational.com</u>)

The Cleft Palate Foundation (<u>www.cleft.com</u>)

Holt International Children's Services (<u>www.holtintl.org</u>)

Wide Smiles (<u>www.widesmiles.org</u>)

0-595-22442-3